Scotland's leading educational publishers

C000179512

Higher
GRAPHIC COMMUNICATION
COURSE NOTES

Higher GRAPHIC COMMUNICATION COURSE NOTES

B Forbes

Table of contents

The contents of this book are guided by the Higher Graphic Communication Course Assessment Specification. You should be aware of the content of this document as it will help you pass the subject.

CONTENTS

8 | The Assessment Standards 158

9 | The Assignment 174

10 | Exam Questions 186

Gaining your qualification

To be awarded a Higher Graphic Communication qualification you must meet all of the assessment standards for the 2D Graphic Communication (Higher) and 3D and Pictorial Graphic Communication (Higher) units.
Once you have gained these units, you will complete the course assessment. The course assessment takes the form of two equally weighted parts: an assignment and an exam.

Meeting the assessment standards

There are different methods that can be used to meet the assessment standards. The Brew Bags project in this book is an example of the type of coursework you could produce in order to pass all of the assessment standards for Higher Graphic Communication.
The Brew Bags project shows how the assessment standards are met naturally through the types of graphic produced when creating a graphic proposal.

The course assignment

You will complete an assessment project given to you by your assessor and set by the SQA. The Tazza Lighting project example in this book is not an SQA set assignment – it is included to show you how you could go about completing the assignment and gain a good mark.

The exam

This book covers everything you need to know to pass the exam. Use the practice papers and SQA past papers to test your understanding and prepare for it.

The assessment standards, course assignment and exam are covered in greater detail towards to back of this book.

This book examines the various aspects of Higher Graphic Communication.

This book provides advice on how to complete the units and the assignment tasks. It does not use the official SQA tasks but the included examples show how you can plan your own work to ensure success within Higher Graphic Communication.

Why is this subject so popular?

The new Graphic Communication courses have been designed to be relevant to the demands of modern industry. The types of graphics you will learn about fall into three categories:

1. Preliminary
2. Production
3. Promotional

These names will not be new to you. You will be familiar with them from the work you completed during National 5. At Higher level, you will be required to produce drawings of a higher quality, using more advanced commands and more in-depth research.

You will develop your ability to produce preliminary graphics when tackling a graphic brief. This includes using a range of techniques to produce high-quality manual graphics.

At the centre of production graphics is 3D modelling. You will use 3D modelling software throughout your studies in this course. This provides you with an industry standard education, so you are excellently prepared for the world of work or university. You will learn many facets of 3D modelling, including different modelling commands and edits, assembly methods and rendering techniques.

You will plan, develop and create a variety of promotional graphics using the design elements and principles of desktop publishing (DTP). You will also develop your knowledge and ability to apply DTP commands in order to produce high-quality presentations.

Once you have developed your skills and knowledge in these areas, you will begin the course assessment. This consists of an assignment (which you will complete in class) and an exam (which you will sit as part of the SQA diet at the end of the year).

The assignment and the exam are worth 70 marks each. The marks are added together to give a total out of 140. The grade you achieve is then calculated by the SQA from the total mark. While the grade boundaries move by one or two marks each year, a general guide is given below:

Grade A: 70% and above
Grade B: 60–69%
Grade C: 50–59%
Grade D: 40–49%

Exam
70 marks

+

Assignment
70 marks

=

Total
140 marks

How to use this book

This book will provide you with all the information you need in order to pass Higher Graphic Communication. It covers all the necessary coursework and contains tips for your assignment and exam.

There are a number of topics that you must know about. The contents page of this book lists these topics. They can also be found in the Course Assessment Specification. This is an important document for the Higher Graphic Communication course and one that your assessor will be familiar with.

This book includes 'Assignment Advice' and 'Exam Tip' boxes throughout. Your final grade for the course is calculated from your marks for the assignment and exam. These boxes identify important points to help you achieve the best marks possible in both.

GO! Assignment Advice

These boxes contain advice to help you complete your assignment.

Course assessment

The course assessment is made up of the assignment and the exam. You must complete the assignment project in class under supervision from your teacher. Your teacher will then mark it out of 70.

The exam is marked out of 70 and is marked externally by the SQA.

Your final award for the course is decided by adding your marks for the assignment and exam together, and calculating a percentage from this.

GO! Exam Tip

These boxes contain hints and tips that will help prepare you for your exam.

Course outline

There are many ways of planning your learning throughout the year. It is a good idea to plan your time so you can structure your learning and ensure you cover all the relevant parts of the course. Your learning plan could look like the one below.

Topic	Jun	Aug	Sep	Oct	Nov	Dec	Jan	Feb	Mar	Apr
Orthographic projection	■									
Sectional Views	■									
Enlarged Views	■									
Assemblies	■									
Exploded Views	■									
Ellipses	■									
Tangency	■									
Interpenetration	■									
Intersections	■									
Surface developments	■									
Auxiliary Views	■									
Tolerances	■									
Building drawings	■									
Pictorial sketching		■								
Manual rendering		■								
3D CAD modelling			■							
CAD drawing techniques			■							
3D CAD assemblies			■							
Computer rendering			■							
Types of promotional graphics					■					
Colour theory					■					
Image types					■					
STP elements & principles					■					
DTP layouts					■					
Assignment based project						■	■			
Assignment									■	
Prelim preperation								■		
Exam preperation									■	

Chapter 1

Types of Graphic

You will learn

- Types of graphic
- Pictorial sketching
- Production graphics
- Promotional graphics

Types of graphic

There are three main types of graphic that are produced during the process of developing new products or engineering solutions. These are:

1. Preliminary graphics

2. Production graphics

3. Promotional graphics

This section provides a brief overview of why and how the different types of graphics are created. The techniques mentioned are covered in more detail later in the book.

Preliminary graphics

Preliminary graphics are initial hand-drawn sketches. These can be produced using traditional methods, such as colour pencils or spirit marker pens.

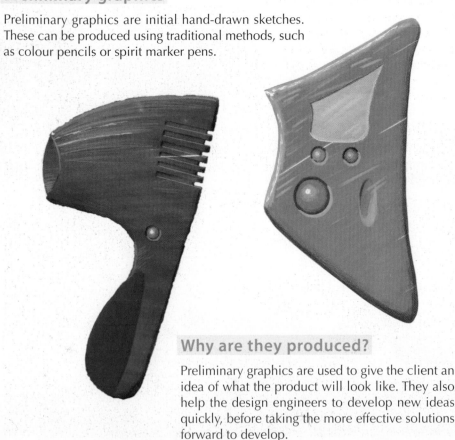

Why are they produced?

Preliminary graphics are used to give the client an idea of what the product will look like. They also help the design engineers to develop new ideas quickly, before taking the more effective solutions forward to develop.

Manual techniques

Using marker pens and colour pencils requires a great deal of skill. Graphic designers use tried and trusted methods to produce 2D images that appear to be 3D.

Highlights and lowlights

Highlights can be used to make it look like light is reflecting from a surface. A white line can be used to show light falling on sharp edges. This effect can be created using white pencils, correction pens or by leaving a gap when marker rendering on white paper.

Lowlights are created using black pencils and show areas of low light and shadows on the sketch.

Tone

Where more layers of a colour are applied, this is called tone. The tonal scale clearly shows this method. It is used to show the gradual change in light in a sketch. It can be used in both pencil and marker pen sketches.

Texture

A graphic designer can indicate different textures where they are proposed to be used.

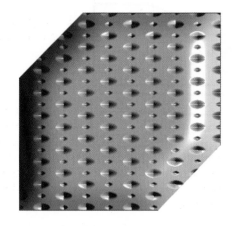

Material

Different materials should be shown to demonstrate where they will be used or combined in an engineering solution. This can be done using a variety of techniques.

Electronic methods of producing preliminary graphics

Modern devices like graphics tablets or touch-screen laptop computers can also be used to produce preliminary graphics. These allow the user to input hand-drawn sketches directly into the computer, without having to master the use of a mouse. This can be used to apply high-quality rendering using computer software. Rendering is the process of showing shape, form, texture and light on an object to make it look realistic. Rendering can be completed using both manual and computer methods – manual during the preliminary stages and computer generated during the promotional stages.

Because these electronic methods allow initial sketches to be produced immediately onto a computer, ideas can be shared quickly through email with anyone in the world. This allows multinational companies to develop and share initial sketches for products from different countries around the world.

Types of sketches

You should be able to sketch using both orthographic and pictorial methods.

Orthographic sketching

When you sketch components orthographically, you have to follow the same drawing conventions you would if using a drawing board. The plan must be projected from the elevation and the end elevation must be projected from the plan.

Orthographic sketches and drawings must project from each other. In other words, the heights, widths and depths must follow each other exactly in each of the views. You can see how the three views of the sharpener are drawn directly above and to the side of one another, with all of the details within the views lining up. This is a vital part of third angle projection. (See page 36 for more information about orthographic sketches and projection.)

It is also good practice to sketch the third angle projection symbol on the sheet to let people know what projection method is being used.

Any dimensions or sectional views must follow British Standard conventions.

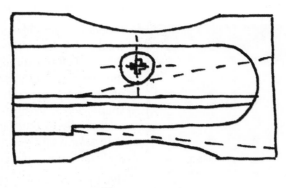

PLAN

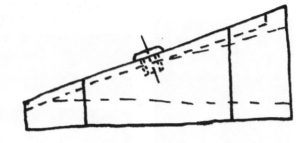

ELEVATION

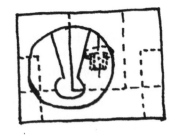

END ELEVATION

Assignment Advice

Practise regularly to ensure your sketches and rendering are of a high quality. For many students, this tends to be the part of the assignment they find most challenging. Practice makes perfect!

Exam Tip

The three drawing areas of preliminary drawings, production drawings and promotional drawings are often referred to as the 3 Ps.

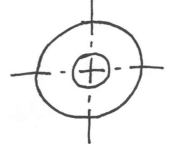

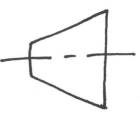

Once the initial sketches have been used to show the design of a product, you need to produce orthographic sketches of the product. These must be dimensioned to show sufficient detail to allow 3D models to be developed.

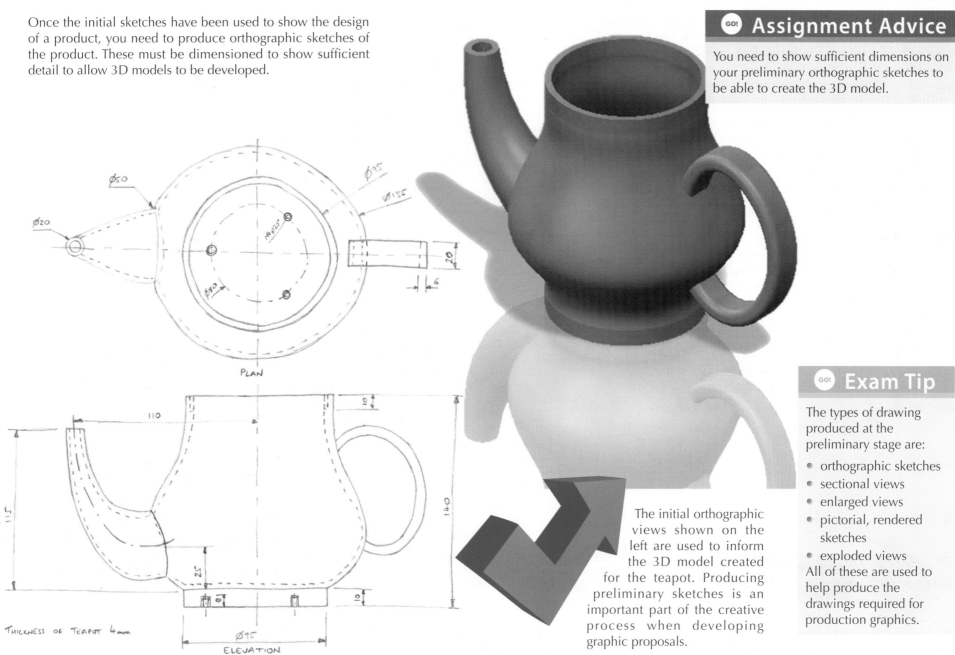

Assignment Advice

You need to show sufficient dimensions on your preliminary orthographic sketches to be able to create the 3D model.

Exam Tip

The types of drawing produced at the preliminary stage are:

- orthographic sketches
- sectional views
- enlarged views
- pictorial, rendered sketches
- exploded views

All of these are used to help produce the drawings required for production graphics.

The initial orthographic views shown on the left are used to inform the 3D model created for the teapot. Producing preliminary sketches is an important part of the creative process when developing graphic proposals.

Pictorial sketching

Your pictorial sketches could include isometric, one-point perspective and two-point perspective methods. You should also show technical detail of how different components of a product fit together using sectional views and/or exploded views where appropriate. These do not have to show the product in its entirety – technical detail can often take the form of an enlarged view to show the relevant parts more clearly.

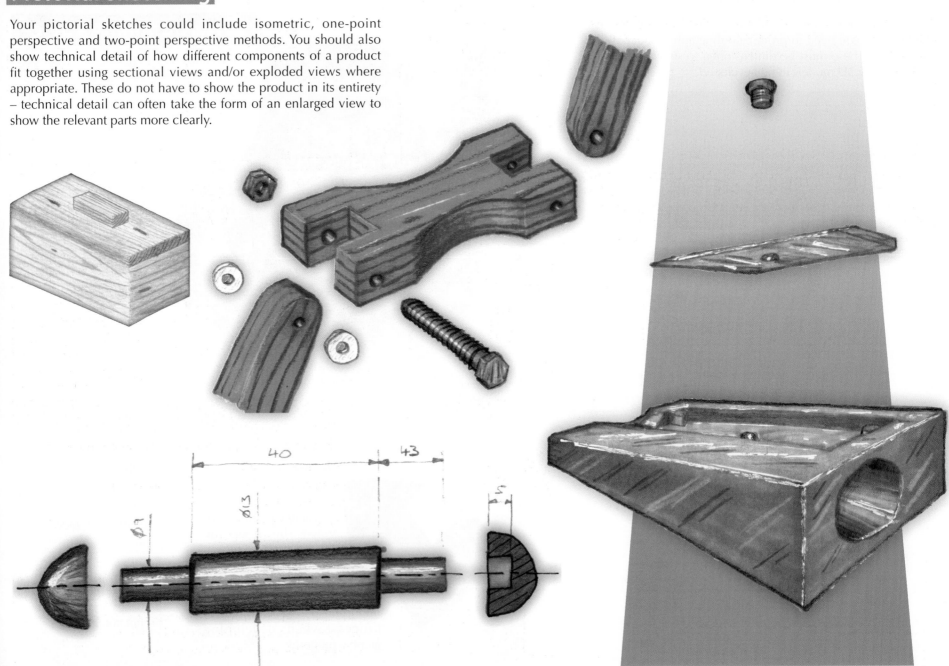

Production graphics

Production graphics are vital for a product or engineering component to be able to be manufactured. They are fully dimensioned and contain technical detail, such as sectional views, enlarged views, component views, exploded views and pictorial views.

Production drawings are often produced from a 3D model created in software. This allows the drawings to be created very quickly. They will also be updated automatically if any changes are made to the 3D model.

It tends to be the orthographic views of the components of an object that have dimensions added to them. This is so that the drawings are clear to understand. Assembly orthographics and pictorial views may include some dimensions, but only those that are vital to understanding how the different parts of an object fit together.

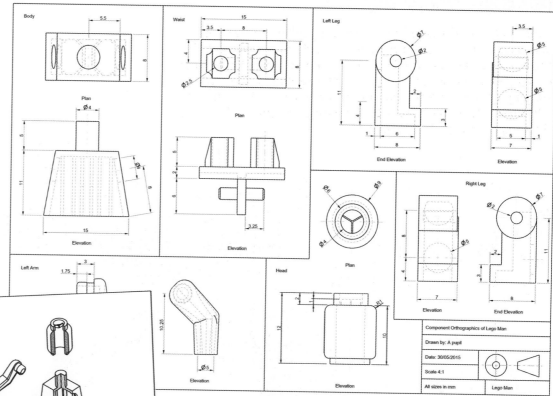

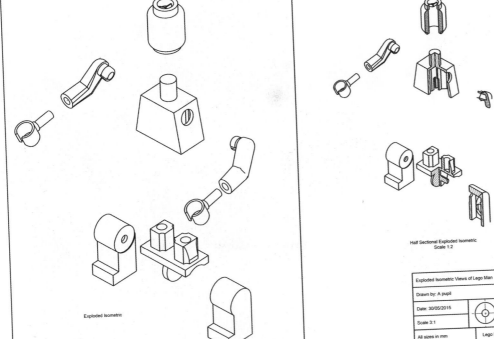

Exam Tip

The types of drawings produced at the production stage are:

- orthographic views
- sectional views, including stepped sections
- enlarged views
- isometric views
- exploded isometric views

Assignment Advice

You have to show dimensioned component orthographics, enlarged views, stepped sections, plus assembled and exploded isometric views in your assignment.

Promotional graphics

Promotional graphics can take a number of different forms:

- magazine articles
- roller banners
- folding leaflets
- table stands
- posters
- web pages
- business cards
- tablet or app display rendered environments

Promotional graphics are used to promote or advertise a product. They should be attractive to look at and must follow some rules and guidelines. These design elements and principles are explained later in this book.

Promotional graphics tend to be produced using DTP software on computers. It is common for there to be standard layouts as part of DTP software. However, you are not allowed to use these in your Higher Graphic Communication course.

Websites and tablet layouts can be animated and have transitions between each of the pages in the structure.

It is commonplace for presentation and rendering software to be used to place 3D rendered models into suitable environments.

Is the importance of handwriting

Falling?

We look into the effects the use of computers is having on our lives.

Handwriting is important because research shows that when children are taught how to do it, they are also being taught how to learn and how to express themselves. A new study to be released this month by Vanderbilt University professor Steve Graham finds that a majority of primary-school teachers believe that students with fluent handwriting produced written assignments that were superior in quantity and quality and resulted in higher grades—aside from being easier to read.

The College Board recognised this in 2005 when it added a handwritten essay to the SAT—an effort to reverse

the de-emphasis on handwriting and composition that may be adversely affecting children's learning all the way through high school and beyond.

How much instruction do kids need in cursive writing? In the 1960s and 1970s, the Zaner-Bloser Co., which has been publishing penmanship curriculum since 1904, recommended 45 minutes a day. By the 1980s, it was suggesting just 15 minutes. Today the average is more like 10 minutes.

Beauty seems to be less important than fluidity and speed. From kindergarten through fourth grade, kids think and write at the same time. (Only later is

Predictions of handwriting's demise didn't begin with the computer, they date back to the introduction of the Remington typewriter in 1873. Now, backed by research, ed wedge the back into th one has sug of the calcu to teach kid is still a prize check. If we it will not or when bride gifts by e-m they'll be co than they af

mental composition divorced from the physical process of handwriting.) If they have to struggle to remember how to make their letters, their ability to express themselves will suffer. The motions have to be automatic, both for expressive writing and for another skill that students will need later in life, note-taking.

Notetaking is an important skill, helped by spending time handwriting.

While modern offices make the use of computers, handwriting is still an essential skill to posses. Learning to write early in life not only helps develop the mechanics but also spelling.

Our latest product

Our new easy-write pen has been scientifically tested to allow ink to flow smoothly through the fine nib.

Independent tests have shown this pen will write for an astonishing 250,000 miles – this is the equivalent of 10 times around the equator.

We are so confident of the quality of our workmanship that this pen also comes with a 25 year guarantee for all moving parts. Refills are also available as we are confident you will never use another pen.

A quality clip allows you to keep the pen in your pocket without fear of losing it.

Our revolutionary fine tip not only allows the writer the freedom of an ultra smooth ink flow but the greatest accuracy of any pen available.

Who are we?

We can supply all of your home and office stationary requirements. Do not hesitate to contact us for expert advice on office layouts or home solutions.

Order a catalogue of our entire range at: www.stationerykings.co.uk

Visit us at:
168 Appleton Street
Sandown
Annesley
AA5 8AQ

STATIONERY Kings

Your one stop shop for all your office needs

STATIONERY Kings

Your one stop shop for all your office needs

STATIONERY Kings
Your one stop shop for all your office needs

We at stationery Kings are proud of our long-standing reputation for quality and aftersales care. We have been the largest supplier of office goods on the east coast of Scotland for many years and are proud of our roots. Stationery Kings is a family run business with over 250 employees working toward giving you the best price and service to help make life easier.

We guarantee to deliver all products to your door within 24 hours and can install our larger items so that you can focus on your business or home activities.

Here, some of our most popular products are displayed. If you would like further information on the items we supply, from desks and chairs to computers and pens, you can contact us and order a catalogue. Our contact details are on the rear of this leaflet.

Thank you for your time and we hope you become another happy customer at Stationery Kings as Stationery Kings helps you with all your stationery needs.

Our promise

Stationery Kings is a family business committed to key principles. These are:

- We supply the highest quality products
- We offer an excellent aftersales service
- We guarantee next day delivery
- We always put customers at the centre of all we do

Computers and electronic devices   Signs and name plates

Office furniture

STATIONERY Kings

Visit us at:
168 Appleton Street
Sandown
Annesley
AA5 8AQ

Your one stop shop for all your office needs

GO! ## Assignment Advice

Save the different versions of your layout as you evaluate it throughout the creative process. You can then annotate the different versions, giving reasons for the changes, to show how the layout has evolved.

TYPES OF GRAPHIC

Chapter 2

Graphic Tools & Techniques

You will learn

- Knowledge and understanding of computer-aided techniques
- Preliminary graphics – manual techniques
- Digital capture/input and output techniques and devices
- Cloud computing
- Image file types
- Features of printed publications
- Digital advertising
- The paperless office
- Remote working
- Safe working practices when using DTP
- The impact of growing DTP software use
- Internet advertising
- CAD animation
- CAD simulation
- 3D printing

Computers have a growing role in the production of the different types of technical drawing needed when designing new products or buildings.

Graphic tablets and stylus pens allow freehand sketching and rendering to be carried out using a computer. 3D computer-aided design (CAD) software allows realistic computer models to be created, edited and tested. Testing can take the form of physical tests. For example, mechanical engineers will test a component to see if it is strong enough for its intended purpose. Tests can also be carried out using virtual reality simulators. For example, in the car industry, they are used to check how many items of luggage will fit into the boot of a car.

All of this means that many checks can be carried out before a physical model has to be made. This speeds up the design process and reduces the costs incurred by a design company.

Promotional drawings are also produced using powerful computer software to give photo-quality renders that can be controlled and edited better than actual photographs. These images can then be imported into a range of advertising publications, to produce a branded package of promotional material to help sell the products or buildings.

Desktop publishing

Many home computers come with DTP packages already installed. A professional standard DTP software package offers the user the ability to produce high-quality DTP documents. Photo editing software can also be used to help prepare images for presentations.

Video editing software can be used to communicate various types of technical graphics to an audience. This can be done using the same principles applied when producing DTP presentations.

Computer-aided design and computer-aided drawing

As 3D CAD packages have evolved and improved over the years with advances in computing technology, the role that this software plays has also changed.

Older 2D computer-aided drawing packages simply allowed a draughtsperson to complete production drawings on a computer using the same techniques as they would have used on a drawing board.

Modern 3D CAD software packages offer the user far more scope for producing and developing a product throughout the graphic design process. CADCAM techniques can be used to manufacture 3D products directly from 3D CAD models. Virtual reality scenarios and animations can be created to show particular technical details of a product, such as how moving parts operate, or to carry out material and strength tests.

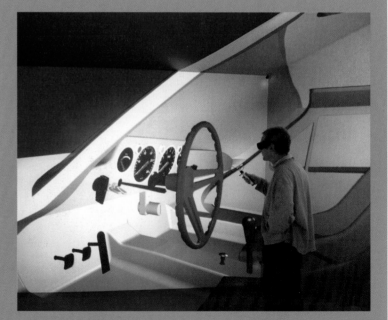

A scientist examines a projection of a Melkus RS 1000 racing car using a 3D CAD model and an interactive virtual reality scene.

Preliminary graphics – manual techniques

It is common for a graphic designer to begin the creative process using manual techniques.

A graphic designer will be able to produce high-quality sketches using the following tools. Indeed, manual techniques can be used to give a very lifelike indication of how a proposed design will look.

GO! Assignment Advice

Practise using these graphic media during your studies to prepare for your assignment.

Often used alongside marker pens, correction pens are a useful and simple tool to create white edges for highlights.

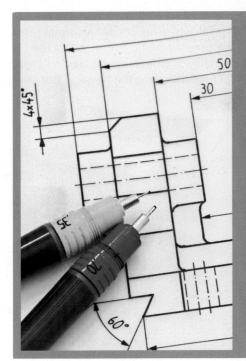

Drawing pens can be used to produce quick sketches and can also be used to add some simple rendering details, shadows and reflections.

Professional graphic design marker pens can be used to render preliminary sketches and give a very realistic image. They are especially useful for showing metals and plastics, but can also be used to show wooden materials.

High-quality graphic design colour pencils are used alongside marker pens to create the finished render. They can also be used on their own to create lifelike renders of an item, so a client can gauge what their product will look like when taken forward through the graphic design process.

Digital capture/input and output techniques and devices

Handheld scanners

Modern handheld scanners are cheap to buy and easy to use. When used properly, they can produce high-quality scans very quickly. Their big advantage over flatbed scanners is that they are portable. They use memory cards to store the images until they can be transferred onto a computer.

Flatbed scanners

Flatbed scanners are useful for producing high-quality scans, as the original image or text is held completely still whilst being scanned. This type of scanner often comes as part of a home inkjet printer.

Laser printers

Laser printers give high-quality printouts using a CMYK format. They are becoming more affordable all the time for home use. Schools tend to use all-in-one copy, scan and print machines, which can be used to create pdf files of paper documents. This can help to reduce the physical storage space required for larger documents.

Graphics tablets

Used with a stylus pen, graphics tablets allow hand-produced sketches to be entered immediately onto a computer. This is far better than using a mouse to sketch and render with. It can be expensive to buy a good quality tablet, but they are coming down in price. Other handheld tablet devices can be used in the same way with rendering apps.

Keyboard

A keyboard is used to input text. It is a basic but essential tool.

Monitor

All of the CAD models and DTP work is displayed on a monitor. When completing graphic projects, a larger, high-resolution monitor is preferable in order to display the images at a high quality.

Mouse

A mouse is needed when using 3D CAD or DTP software. The middle button on the mouse is a vital tool when using CAD, so it is important that you use a mouse that has one. (Any good quality computer mouse will have one.)

Projector

Projectors can be used to display work, animations or videos on a large screen to allow lots of people to view them.

Drum plotter

Drum plotters allow large drawings to be printed. The paper is moved back and forth through the printer by rollers. The printer head, which uses pens to produce line drawings, moves along the motorised axis.

Wide format inkjet printers like the one shown below allow large images to be printed for posters or banners. The rolls of paper used can be very long and the width of paper is limited by the size of the drum, which can be up to a few metres wide.

Sublimation printers

Sublimation printers can be used to print onto a variety of materials. They can be used to print onto a substrate, which can then be heat pressed onto soft advertising banners, T-shirts, rulers and mugs amongst other items.

The sublimation printer shown on the right can be used to print a graphic that can then be transferred onto 3D items, such as mugs.

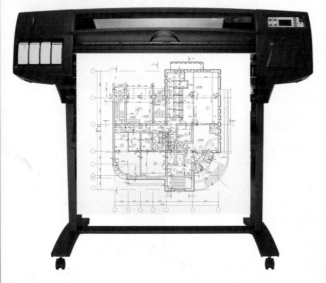

Portable storage facilities

Portable storage devices include USB flash drives and portable hard drives. They allow the user to save their work, take it with them and open the files on any computer in order to continue their work or to showcase it to others.

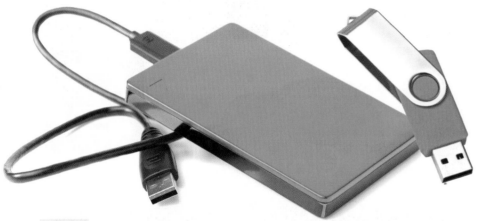

Email

Email can be used to share files immediately with anyone else anywhere in the world. Anyone with Internet access has free email services available to them, making this a time-efficient and environmentally friendly method of communication.

Cloud storage

Cloud storage offers the user a method of storing their work without having the need for any physical storage devices. Cloud storage has the added benefit of giving the user access to their work from any computer in the world that is connected to the Internet. The amount of cloud storage offered by companies differs, but can be large enough to suit any individual or organisation.

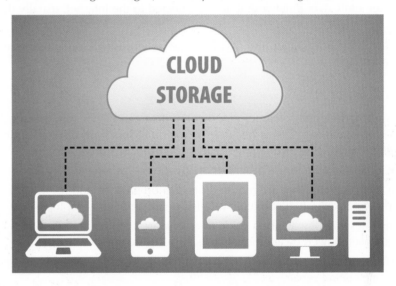

Cloud storage also provides a useful method of backup storage. It can be set to automatically sync with the contents of a hard drive or network to prevent data loss through disk or system corruption.

There are many different cloud storage options and some people will choose to keep the different types of files they have with different companies to improve their personal online security.

Cloud computing

Cloud computing has many uses and is improving as the technology that supports it improves. In computing, the term 'cloud' means 'Internet', so this is all about using computer programs over the Internet.

Traditionally, any programs or files that a user runs on their computer would have to have been installed onto their computer first.

This is called local storage and computing. Cloud computing allows programs to be run remotely over a network that is connected to the Internet, usually through WIFI.

There are some advantages and disadvantages when using cloud computing and cloud apps:

Advantages

- Computers designed solely for cloud computing can be cheaper than desktop or laptop machines. This is because they require less hard drive memory for programs and files as everything is either run from, or stored onto, the cloud.
- Individuals are able to use programs on any device, wherever they are.
- Only the programs that are required need to be paid for and used, instead of the other packages that come preinstalled on a computer or laptop.
- Companies can pay a subscription to a software producer rather than a large initial cost followed by additional costs for software updates.
- The most up-to-date version of the software will always be available as it is run from one central server.

Disadvantages

- A fast and reliable Internet connection is required to run cloud computing apps. A slow or inconsistent Internet connection will make cloud computing challenging.
- Connection charges to high-speed Internet connections can be expensive. This is especially true for companies who rely on this service. They can spend lots of money on their connection as any downtime from the Internet will lead to a lack of productivity.
- There can also be issues over who owns the rights to anything created or stored in the cloud.

At this time, cloud computing is still in its infancy. Lots of technological developments will take place to improve this service with time and investment. Some schools are investing in cloud computing so that each student can work with a computer in every classroom. Some companies are already successfully using cloud computing systems. It allows portable access to apps as long as there is an Internet connection.

Image file types

There are two main file types for images: raster files and vector files. Each type has its own advantages and disadvantages.

Raster graphics (tiff, jpg, png, bmp, gif, psd)

Raster graphics are created using a series of coloured pixels or squares. They can be created and edited using photo editing packages. They tend to be used for photographs and similar images.

Advantages

- low file size
- easy to use
- can be edited using common photo editing programs

Disadvantages

- images can become pixelated
- can be less suitable for high-quality print material, especially large print projects

Vector graphics (svg, dxf, eps, ai, cdr)

Vector graphics use mathematically defined areas to produce the shapes contained within the image. They can only be created by professional DTP and photo editing software, such as Serif DrawPlus or Adobe Illustrator.

Advantages

- can be use to create laser cutter tool paths
- can be resized without a loss of sharpness
- clear and precise graphics can be produced

Disadvantages

- cannot be used for photographs
- only specialised software packages can be used to edit these type of graphics
- software for editing vector graphics can be expensive (although some packages can be downloaded free of charge)

> ### GO! Exam Tip
>
> You are likely to be asked to compare raster and vector files and to identify why one would be used in place of another in a given scenario.

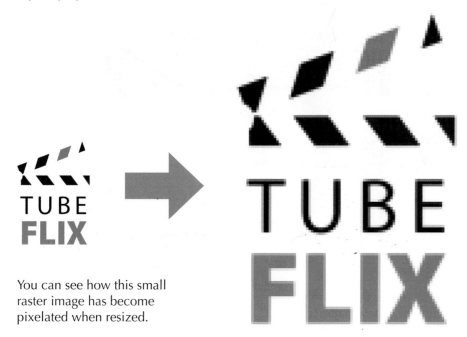

You can see how this small raster image has become pixelated when resized.

When this svg file is resized, there is no loss of sharpness.

Features of printed publications

When printing on a commercial scale, it is important to be able to check if the process is set up properly and the printing machines are printing accurately. In order to do that a number of check marks are printed at the side of the paper, outside the publication. These will be trimmed off before the publication is bound.

Register marks

Registration is the name given to creating perfectly matched, overlapping colours on a page. When printing using the CMYK method, there will be a CMYK printing register mark visible, which allows it to be checked.

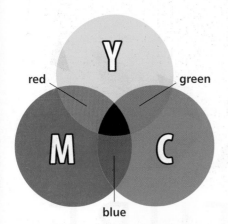

red   green

blue

Colour printing typically uses ink of four colours: cyan, magenta, yellow and key (black).

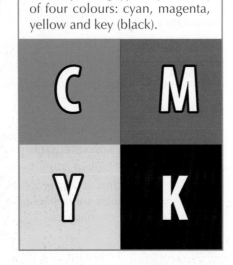

CMYK refers to the four layers of colour that are applied separately in the printing process. It stands for cyan, magenta, yellow and key (black). The colours must be aligned properly otherwise the printed images will appear distorted.

When two of the CMY 'primaries' are combined, the resulting 'secondary' mixtures are red, green and blue. If all three are combined, black is produced.

Key (or black) ink is used to save ink, as combining the other three colours is an inefficient method of producing back.

When the registration is perfectly matched then the register mark will be clear and precise. When it is not, then the coloured circles will be printed in different places.

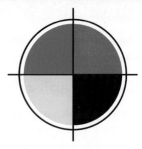

You can see how the registration mark on the left is misaligned, indicating a mistake in the application of the CMYK layers.

Colour bars

Colour bars are printed outside the trim area and are used to check the quality of the colours being printed in the document.

Crop marks

Crop marks are small marks at the corners of the finished page that show where the paper should be trimmed before binding. The term 'bleed area' describes the part of the paper outside the crop marks to which images or features are printed. This ensures that these features are printed to the full extent of the finished page. The bleed area is removed when the pages are trimmed before binding.

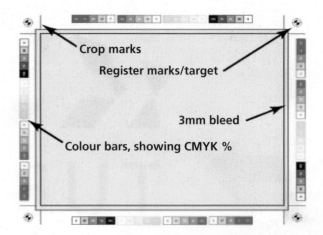

Crop marks

Register marks/target

3mm bleed

Colour bars, showing CMYK %

Print run

The print run is the number of copies of a newspaper or magazine that are printed at one time.

GO! Exam Tip

Your exam will cover real world applications of graphics and producing printed work. Questions on registration marks and other printing features are likely to be included.

Digital advertising

Many adverts are displayed using digital formats. These digital adverts can be shown in a variety of places, from football stadiums to bus stops, using permanent or portable displays.

Digital adverts offer many different advantages to advertisers:

- It is environmentally friendly to display promotional layouts on digital displays as ink and paper are not required.
- Adverts can be changed regularly, cheaply and quickly.
- Adverts can use moving images to attract attention.
- Different adverts can be shown on the same display and flip through to have greater impact and advertise more products.
- Displays can be emailed to different venues, cutting down on delivery costs.

There are also some drawbacks to these digital platforms:

- The displays use electricity.
- Digital boards have to be transported around the country to allow the promotional work to be displayed.
- Consumers cannot take a hard copy of these adverts home for reference at a later date.

GO! Exam Tip

With the widespread presence of mobile phones and tablets, and the increasing amount of digital advertising space becoming available, digital advertising is a large and modern area of graphic communication and, as such, is likely to feature in your exam.

The paperless office

One of the major benefits to industry and the environment of the use of computers, DTP software and the Internet has been the reduction in paper used. Important documents are saved onto disk and held on computer systems.'

For DTP workplaces, this can be applied to almost all the work produced. Very little work is now produced by hand during the process of developing professional DTP publications. Thumbnail layouts are produced by computer software as it is quicker and allows high-quality work to be quickly produced all the way through the DTP development process, using structured grids and layouts.

Companies that can reduce the amount of paper used in their day-to-day work will save money and increase profit margins.

GO! Exam Tip

Revise the impact of the paperless office and remote working when preparing for your exam.

Remote working

DTP work can be shared immediately through the use of email systems. Employees can work from home or in separate offices on the same item of work.

Storing data on a single drive or server allows different people, in different places, to work on and update the same document. This allows companies to have international offices working on documents simultaneously to increase production and make use of the skills of a varied workforce.

All of this means that companies can become global as the world becomes connected via electronic, mobile and satellite networks. Anyone, from anywhere in the world, can communicate with anyone else using a variety of platforms.

Many news platforms and magazines are Internet based and rely on DTP work to make their content look appealing. This opens exciting new markets and opportunities for a new range of employment prospects in this business sector.

Safe working practices when using DTP

If a business is to use DTP all day to produce documents, the welfare of their employees has to be protected.

Ergonomic factors have to be considered to look after a person's physical wellbeing. Ensuring that adjustable seating and footstools are provided and that wrist rests are used is essential.

Offices must be suitably lit with non-glare lighting and regular breaks must be taken from the computer screen to avoid headaches and eye strain. Other factors that have to be considered are tidy workspaces and arranging hardware and cables safely.

The impact of growing DTP software use

The introduction of DTP and computers has had a massive impact on the graphic communication industry and on the environment.

Since their introduction in design offices, computers have completely transformed the industry. Offices can now be paperless, with the use of graphics tablets, email, digital cameras and editing suites. In addition, the time it takes to produce publications has been shortened with the increased ease of editing through the use of computer software.

This has also been extended to the use of home computers and people creating their own DTP items, from calendars to cards.

There are a wide variety of DTP packages available to use. Some are shown here.

Serif
Inspiring Creativity

PagePlus X9
The Ultimate Desktop Publisher

GO! Exam Tip

Revise the impact of the introduction and development of DTP software when preparing for your exam.

GRAPHIC TOOLS AND TECHNIQUES

31

Internet advertising

Most websites sell advertising space on their pages to generate income. These use the same graphic elements and principles as promotional material.

Website designers code the page to add links and create flashing or moving images to attract the attention of users. The presentation of the adverts is produced by a graphic designer for the website designer to use.

The most useful feature of advertising on websites is that web designers can use the information stored on your computer, phone or tablet to tailor the adverts you see. For example, if you have been searching for jackets, you will often be able to see adverts for jackets on the websites you are visiting. This is obviously a huge advantage for advertisers and is why graphic design plays a large part in website design.

CAD animation

Computer animation can be used to help communicate how the moving parts of a 3D CAD model work together.

Animations allow a user to see how a product looks or moves. They are played and watched with no other input from the user.

Animations are used as a communication tool rather than a testing tool for the product. They are very useful in the promotional stages of a graphic presentation. The client will often wish to see an animated video to understand how moving parts work or how the various parts of an assembly are placed together.

GO! Exam Tip

Animation: the user simply watches it and cannot affect the outcome.

Simulation: the user interacts with the software, which allows different outcomes depending on what the user does.

CAD simulation

Simulations allow the user to interact with a product. The outcome of the simulation is dependent on the user's input. For example, a flight simulator can be used to train pilots without the risk of crashing a plane.

Simulations can also be used to test the strength of a product. Once a CAD model has had a material applied to it, the relevant part of the model will take on the engineering properties of that material. A load can then be applied to the model and the stress and strain measured and displayed. This is advantageous for a number of reasons:

- products can be tested for strength without lots of expensive physical models being tested to destruction
- changes to the design to strengthen failing parts can be made immediately
- a large number of different physical factors can be controlled, such as the temperature of the material and wind strength.

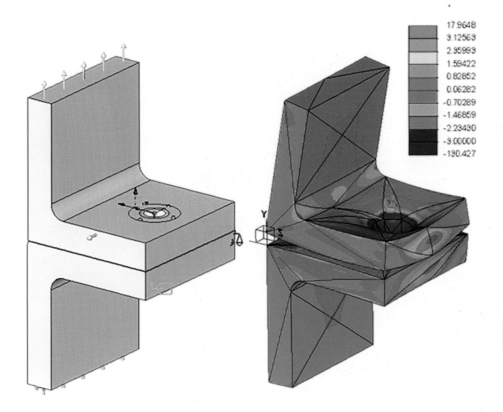

17.9648
3.12563
2.35993
1.59422
0.82852
0.06282
-0.70289
-1.46859
-2.23430
-3.00000
-180.427

3D printing

3D printing is a growing area of the design process, which is having a large impact on manufacture. There is almost no limit to what can be produced using a 3D printer straight from a drawing. A variety of items, from tiny objects to buildings, are being produced using 3D printing techniques. Complex items with moving parts can be printed overnight and examined to see how they work quickly and easily, speeding up a traditionally time-consuming part of the design process.

Some companies are producing products to sell by 3D printing them. This reduces manufacturing costs for the companies involved. Once the 3D printer has been purchased, it can print any shape without any expensive tooling requirements.

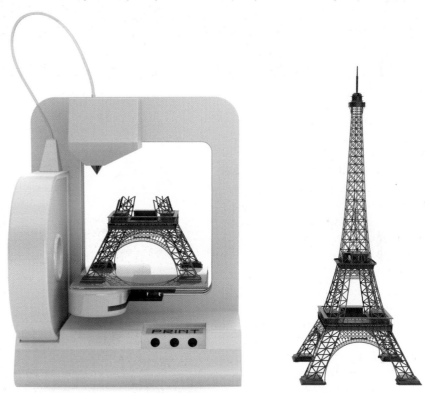

🔵 GO! Exam Tip

Rapid prototyping techniques, such as 3D printing, speed up the design process. The size of object that can be produced using 3D printing techniques is dependent on the size of the 3D printer.

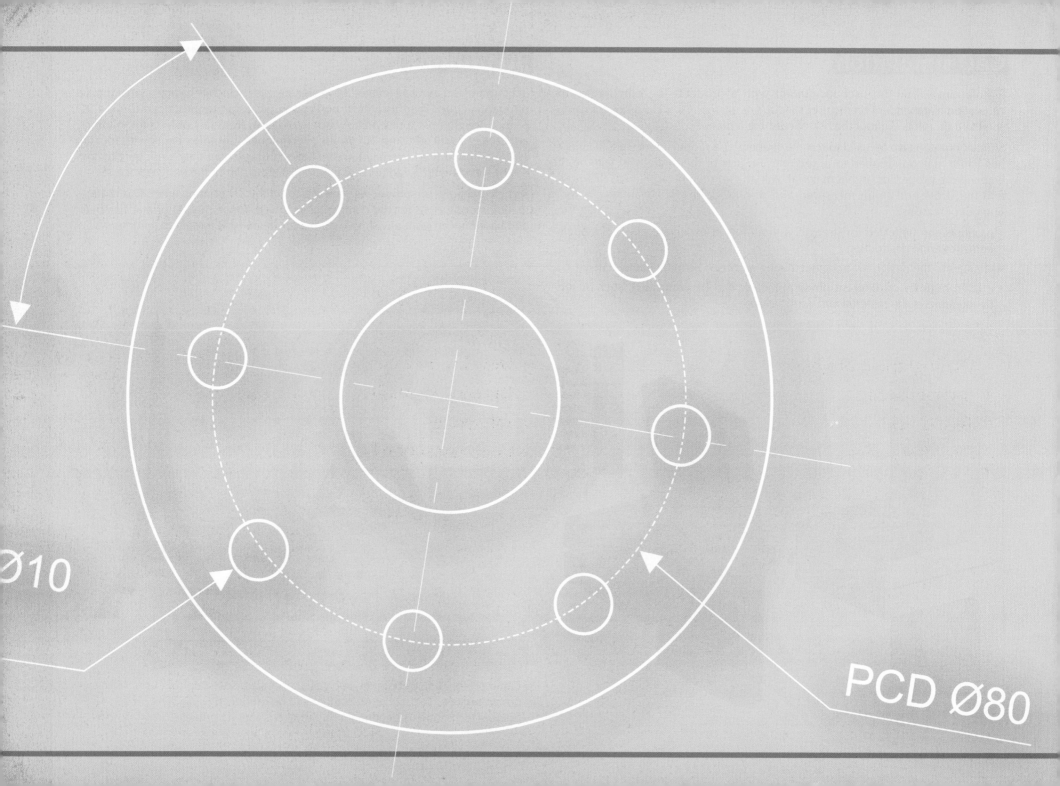

Ø10

PCD Ø80

Chapter 3

Drawing, Dimensioning & Symbols

You will learn

- Orthographic projection
- Dimensioning
- Title block
- Drawing scales

- Drawing sets
- Drawing symbols
- Tolerances
- Common symbols

Orthographic projection

When laying out orthographic drawings, drawing standards should be consistently applied. In schools, the method used is third angle projection.

Third angle projection

It is vital to show the third angle projection symbol on any drawing work you do, so that people reading the drawing know what projection method has been used.

Orthographic projection is a way of drawing different views of an object. In third angle projection, the plan (top view) is drawn directly above the elevation (front view) and the end elevation (side view) is drawn directly to the right of the elevation.

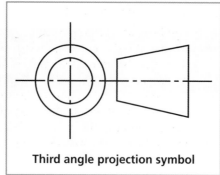

Third angle projection symbol

The drawing below shows how a third angle projection brings the three views together.

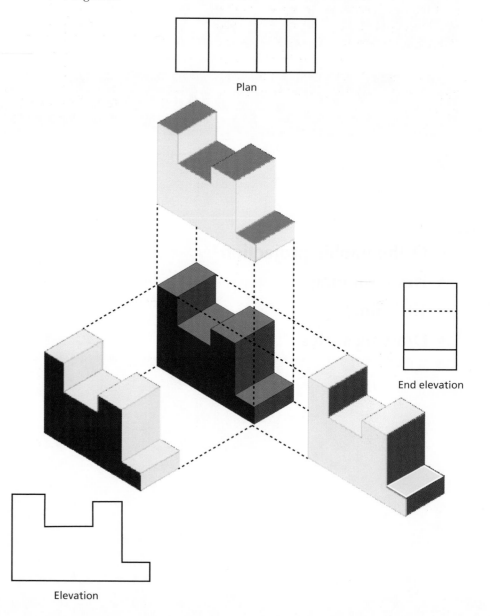

Plan

End elevation

Elevation

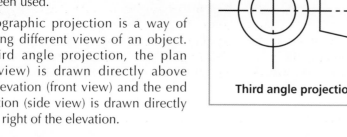

Plan

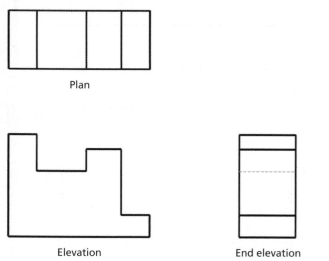

Elevation

End elevation

First angle projection

First angle projection is not used within Higher Graphic Communication, but you should be aware that it exists. It is the opposite of third angle projection. The plan is shown below the elevation and the right-hand side view (end elevation) is shown on the left.

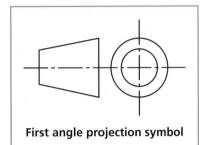

First angle projection symbol

End elevation

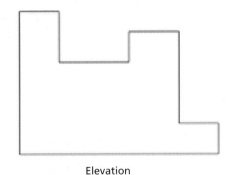

Elevation

Plan

Line types

You need to know the different line types that are used in orthographic drawings.

The lines are all drawn to British Standards so that they can be understood by anyone who reads the drawing. This eliminates mistakes that could be expensive to fix or, more importantly, dangerous if translated to the end product.

Construction line	
Outline	
Hidden detail line	
Centre line	
Fold line	
Cutting plane	A ↓ A ↓
Line of symmetry	

Dimensioning

Vertical dimensions are always written in the middle and on the left-hand side of the dimension line.

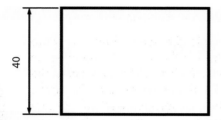

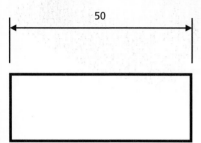

Horizontal dimensions are always written in the middle and above the dimension line.

Chain dimensioning

Chain dimensions follow each other in a line.

Auxiliary dimensions

Auxiliary dimensions are not required on a drawing for any technical reason, but help to make lengths more obvious.

GO! Assignment Advice

You must use the correct British Standards method of dimensioning for both your preliminary and production drawings.

This is an example of an auxiliary dimension.

Chain dimensioning is used to show the length of each step in this shape.

Parallel dimensioning

Parallel dimensions are shown above and below each other. They are used when dimensioning from a datum point. The advantage of using this type of dimensioning is that it is more accurate when tolerances are important.

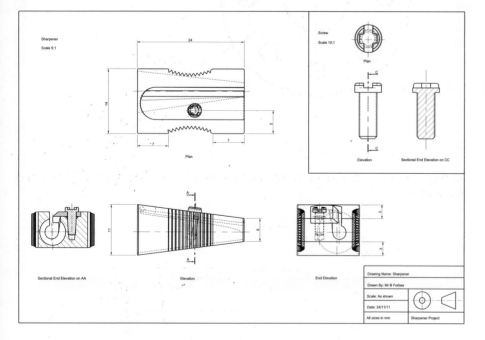

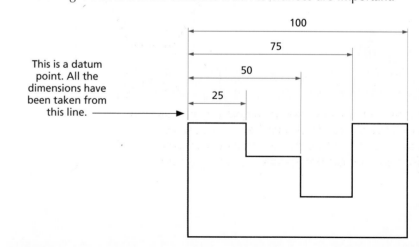

This is a datum point. All the dimensions have been taken from this line.

Running dimensioning

Running dimensions show the sizes from the datum line. The values are not positioned in the centre of the dimension line in this method, to help show that all the dimensions are taken from the datum line. It also helps to differentiate running dimensions from the other methods.

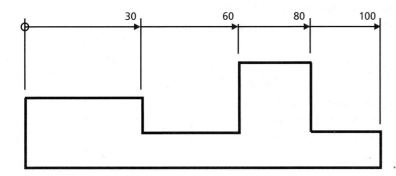

Pitch circle diameter

Pitch circle diameter allows a group of circles on the same diameter to be dimensioned clearly. The diameter of the circle that all the circles sit on is shown, as is the diameter of each individual circle and the angles between the circles.

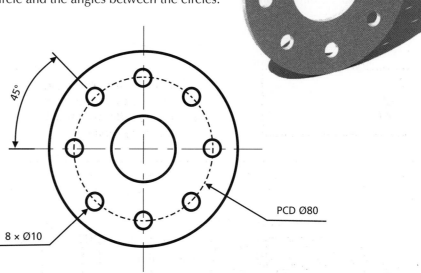

Angular dimensioning

Angles need to be dimensioned to show their slope. This is important to allow tapered objects to be manufactured accurately.

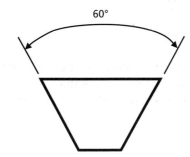

Dimensioning an ellipse

An ellipse has two different measurements to be dimensioned: the major axis and minor axis.

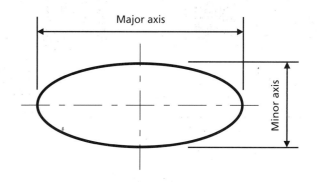

Dimensioning a circle

There are three acceptable methods you can use to dimension a circle. You should choose the most suitable one for the drawing you are dimensioning. Remember that the purpose of dimensions is to clearly show the technical details of a drawing, so you should pick the method that allows you do do this. This symbol Ø means diameter and must be positioned before the numerical size whenever you are dimensioning a circle.

A circle can be dimensioned using an arrow that passes through the centre of the circle.

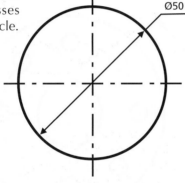

A circle can be dimensioned using leader lines and either a horizontal or vertical arrow.

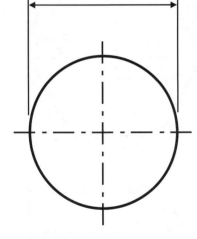

A circle can be dimensioned using an arrow on the outside of the circle. This arrow must be in line with the centre of the circle.

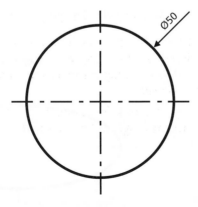

Dimensioning a radius

There are two ways of dimensioning a radius. As with dimensioning circles, you should choose the method that most clearly shows the radius. The symbol R is used to show a radius.

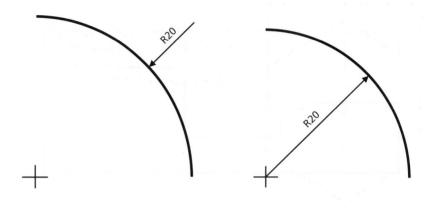

Dimensioning small features

When dimensioning small features, placing the dimension arrow between projection lines may create a drawing that is difficult to read. In order to clarify the dimensions of small features, any of the methods shown below can be used.

Dimensioning a hexagon

There are two ways that hexagons can be dimensioned: either across the faces (AF) or across the corners (AC).

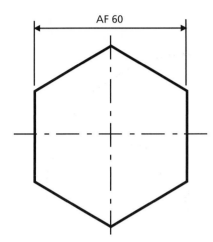

AF 60

The British Standards symbol for across the faces is AF. The number indicates the size of the hexagon in millimetres.

AF 60

Ø60

30°

When drawing a hexagon using manual methods, you start by using a pair of compasses to draw a circle.

If the hexagon is dimensioned across the faces, then it is drawn outside the circle.

If the hexagon is dimensioned across the corners, then the hexagon is drawn inside the circle.

AC 80

60°

Ø80

The British Standards symbol for across the corners is AC. The number indicates the size of the hexagon.

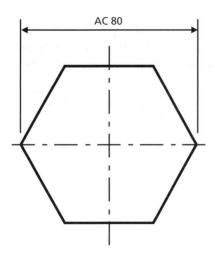

AC 80

Dimensioning a square

As all the sides of a square are of equal length, there is a British Standards convention to apply that makes dimensioning a square more efficient and clearer to read.

The □ symbol identifies a square, while the number identifies the length of the sides of the square.

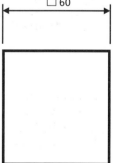

□ 60

DRAWING, DIMENSIONING & SYMBOLS

Title block

A title block is a label added to a drawing that contains relevant information. This information is needed to be able to read production drawings properly, so that the product they are showing can be manufactured.

A title block should contain:

1. The name of the drawing.

2. The name of the person who produced the drawing.

3. The date the drawing was produced on.

4. The scale of the drawing.

5. The projection symbol.

6. The unit of measurement used for the drawing.

7. The title of the project.

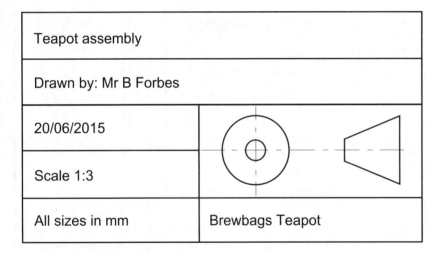

Teapot assembly	
Drawn by: Mr B Forbes	
20/06/2015	
Scale 1:3	
All sizes in mm	Brewbags Teapot

GO! Exam Tip

You need to be able to identify the details found in a title block and know how to work out scales for drawings.

Drawing scales

Drawing scales are used regularly in drawing sets. They tell you how much smaller or larger a drawing is than the real life object.

They can be calculated very easily. A scale of 2:1 means double size, while a scale of 1:2 is half size. To work it out, replace the colon (:) with a dividing line. For example:

2:1 becomes $\frac{2}{1}$ which means the size is doubled.

1:2 becomes $\frac{1}{2}$ which means the size is halved.

When an object is shown at full size, the scale is 1:1.

There are three main factors that affect the scale used for an object:

1. The size of the paper the object is drawn on.

2. The size of the object itself.

3. The amount of detail needed to be shown.

Often you will see enlargement scales of 50:1, 20:1 and 2:1.

You will also see reduction scales of 1:50, 1:200 and 1:1250 used in building sets for floor plans, site plans and location plans respectively.

Use of appropriate drawing scales

Different items will have to be drawn at a range of different scales. You have to be able to select the most relevant scale for your needs.

Larger items will need to be drawn at smaller scales, while smaller items often have to be scaled up to clearly see the detail.

The size of the paper used to produce a drawing is also a contributing factor in selecting the scale. Larger sheets of paper allow a larger drawing to be printed than smaller sheets.

The drawing below shows the parts of a lamp drawn at different scales in order to show the detail in them. This allows the engineer to view the smaller and larger parts of the lamp clearly, so that it can be manufactured.

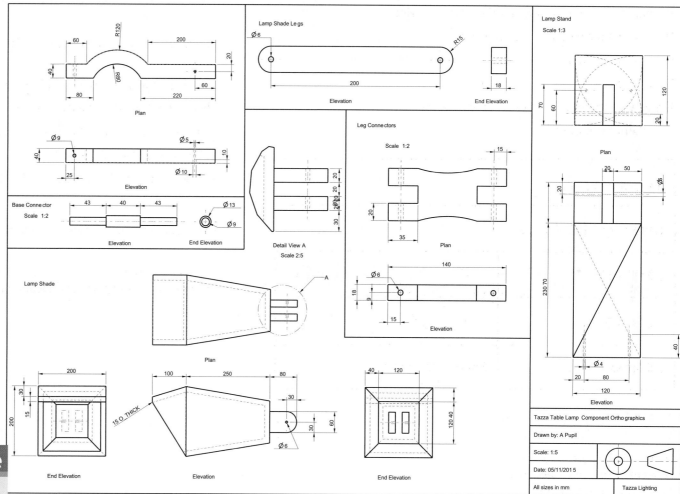

Assignment Advice

Scales should be shown for the production drawings you produce. Select appropriate scales to clearly show the details of your solution.

Drawing sets

Drawing sets contain all the drawings necessary to complete a building project. A drawing set will include drawings to clearly show the layout of the buildings and where they will be situated.

There are three drawings used to show this. These are listed below along with the scale they are drawn at:

1. Location plan – 1:1250

2. Site plan – 1:200

3. Floor plan – 1:50

> ### GO! Exam Tip
>
> Make sure you know the scales used for floor plans, site plans and location plans.

Location plan

A location plan shows the position of a building within a wider area. Surrounding streets and buildings are shown.

Site plan

A site plan shows where a building is going to be built and its immediate surrounding area. Some of the details shown in a site plan are:

- drainage
- gas pipe work
- electrical supply cables
- telephone and TV cables
- trees and hedges
- slopes (called swales) to take rainwater away from the house.

Below is an example of a site plan. The arrow within the circle is the symbol used to indicate the direction of north on a map.

> ### GO! Exam Tip
>
> You will need to know the symbols for these items for your exam.

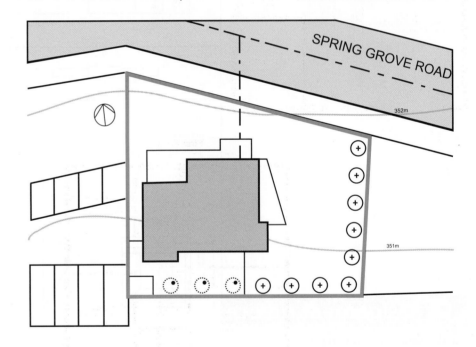

Floor plan

A floor plan shows the details of a layout of the floor in a building. Walls, windows, doors, sockets, switches, lamps, furniture and staircases are some of the items shown using this layout.

Ground Floor
Approx. 83.4 sq. metres (897.8 sq. feet)

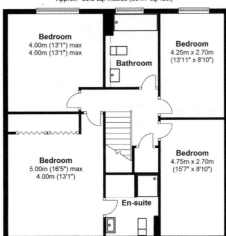

First Floor
Approx. 80.3 sq. metres (864.7 sq. feet)

Throughout these drawing sets you must use the correct British Standard symbols for any detail or item you show in them.

You will have access to a document produced by the SQA that contains all of the symbols that you need to know for all levels of Graphic Communication study. This document is called 'Graphic Communication – Standards and Conventions' and is available to download from the SQA website for Higher Graphic Communication.

The terms used in this book for the British Standard signs and symbols, as defined by the SQA, are correct at the time of going to print. It may be worth checking the SQA website for any updates when you are revising this part of the course.

It is imperative that you use only the terms and words stated in the SQA book for each of the items.

Exam Tip

You must state the exact term used by British Standards for these symbols in order to be awarded the marks in the exam. The reference book produced by the SQA contains the correct names.

Drawing symbols are used in plans for buildings. They allow the materials and details of a building to be communicated to builders and engineers. They follow British Standards and are always drawn the same way so that people can understand them.

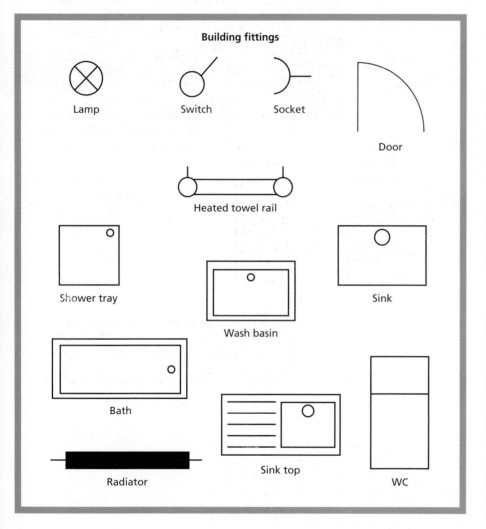

Building fittings

Lamp

Switch

Socket

Door

Heated towel rail

Shower tray

Wash basin

Sink

Bath

Sink top

WC

Radiator

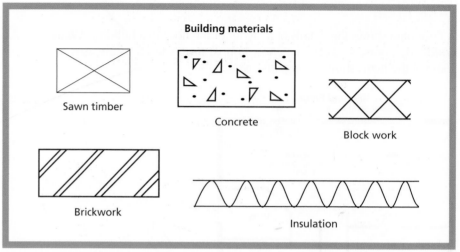

Building materials

Sawn timber

Concrete

Block work

Brickwork

Insulation

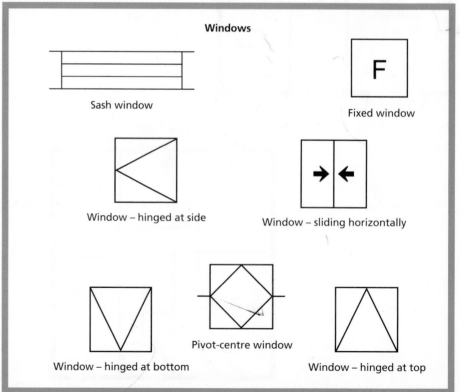

Windows

Sash window

Fixed window

Window – hinged at side

Window – sliding horizontally

Window – hinged at bottom

Pivot-centre window

Window – hinged at top

If asked to identify these symbols in your exam, you must use the exact terms given here in order to be awarded the marks.

Site plan symbols

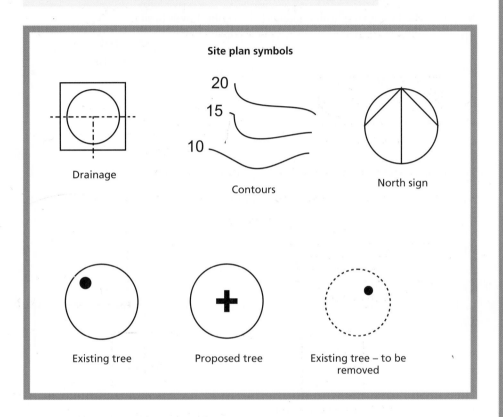

Drainage

Contours

North sign

Existing tree

Proposed tree

Existing tree – to be removed

Engineering symbols

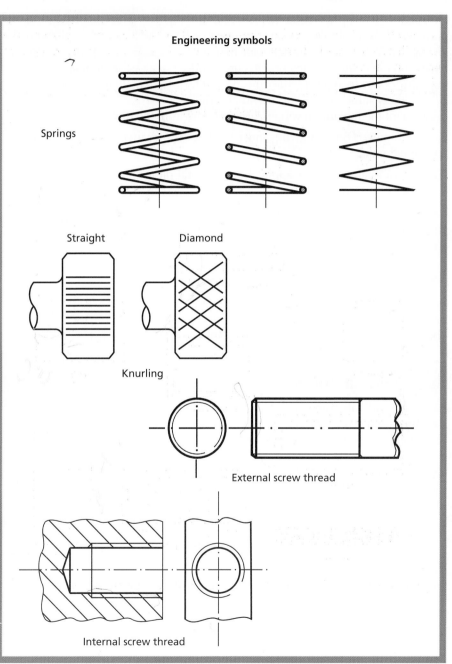

Springs

Straight

Diamond

Knurling

External screw thread

Internal screw thread

Tolerances

In practice, it is not possible to manufacture products to the exact dimensions displayed on an engineering drawing. The accuracy depends largely on the manufacturing process used and the care taken to manufacture the product. A tolerance value shows the manufacturing department the maximum variation permissible from the dimension.

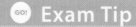

GO! Exam Tip

Take a calculator into your exam to help calculate tolerances.

Each dimension on a drawing must include a tolerance value. This can appear either as:

- a general tolerance value applicable to several dimensions, e.g. General Tolerance ± 0.5 mm
- a tolerance specific to that dimension.

There are two methods of tolerancing dimensions. These are symmetrical and asymmetrical tolerances.

Symmetrical tolerances

Symmetrical tolerances are used in instances when the dimensions of the manufactured object can be out by the same amount above or below the dimensioned size.

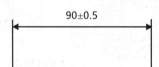

Asymmetrical tolerances

Asymmetrical tolerances are used when a size must be between two given dimensions. Note the comma used in the tolerance sizes.

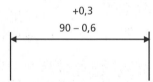

Tolerancing of individual linear dimensions

When it is important that individual dimensions are toleranced over and above the general tolerance for an object, the tolerance should be written as shown below. This shows the minimum and maximum sizes for the part clearly.

Note that the larger size limit is placed above the lower limit.

All tolerances should be expressed to the appropriate number of decimal places for the degree of accuracy intended from manufacturing, even if the value is a zero. For example:

- 45·25 should be expressed as 45,25
- 44·8 should be expressed as 44,80

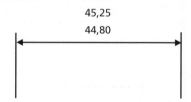

Functional and non-functional tolerances

Functional tolerances are essential to a component being manufactured correctly. The sizes indicated by these must be accurate for the product or part to work properly.

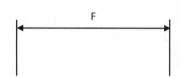

Non-functional tolerances are not as important as they do not play a critical role in the function of a part.

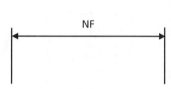

Common symbols

Using symbols to convey information is the crux of Graphic Communication. Using graphics to inform people has many advantages over literary methods. Information can be understood far quicker and people of any nationality can understand the message when it is communicated graphically.

Symbols are not restricted to engineering contexts. Storyboards can be produced to help people understand how something works. For example, how to operate a machine or toy. Road signs used across the UK since 1965 were developed by Margaret Calvert and Jock Kinneir to quickly convey information while the viewer is moving.

Types of signs

A mandatory sign

A prohibition sign

A warning sign

A safe condition sign

The BSI kite mark

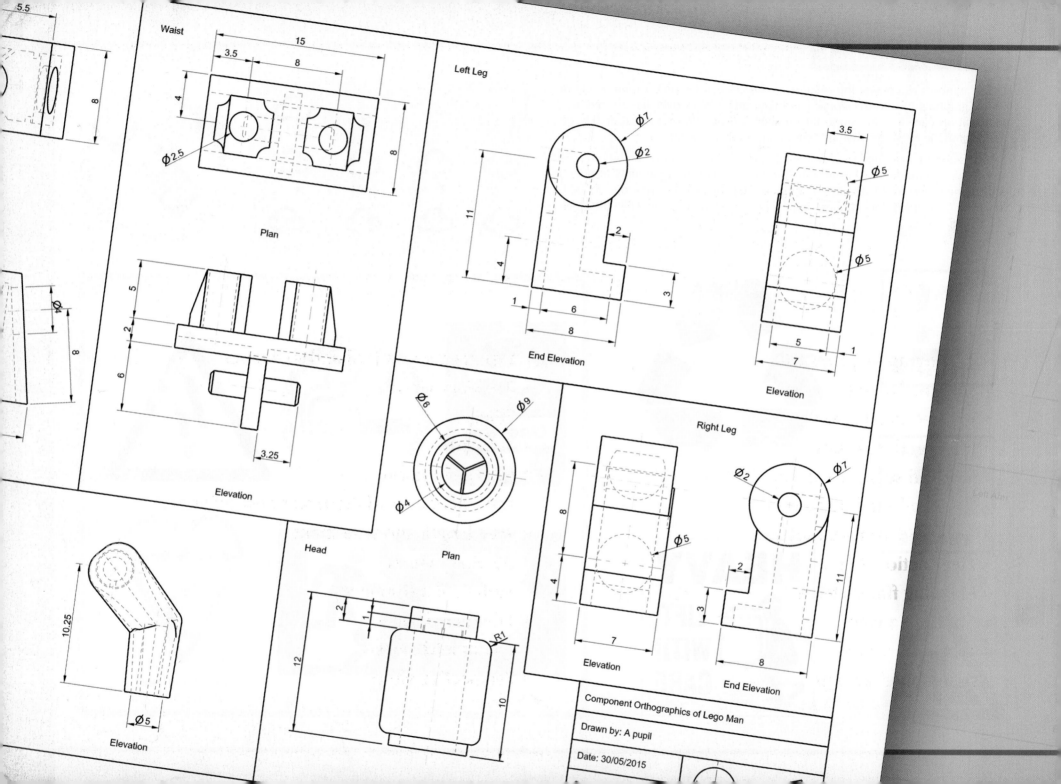

Waist

5.5

8

15
3.5
8
4
8
Ø2.5

Plan

5
2
6
3.25

Elevation

Ø4
8

Left Leg

Ø7
Ø2

11
4
2
3
1
6
8

End Elevation

3.5
Ø5
Ø5
5
1
7

Elevation

Head

Ø6
Ø9
Ø4

Plan

10.25
Ø5

Elevation

2
1
12
R1
10

Right Leg

8
4
Ø5
7

Elevation

Ø2
Ø7
2
3
11
8

End Elevation

Component Orthographics of Lego Man

Drawn by: A pupil

Date: 30/05/2015

Chapter 4

Technical Drawings

You will learn

- Orthographic projection
- Sectional views
- Full sectional views
- Half-sectional views
- Stepped sectional views
- Revolved sectional views
- Removed sectional views
- Part-sectional views
- Showing flat surfaces
- Showing a web
- Isometric views
- Assembly drawings

- Exploded views (full and sectional)
- Auxiliary views
- Ellipses
- Tangency
- Interpenetration
- Intersections of right prisms and cylinders
- True length and true shape
- Auxiliary views
- Surface development
- Oblique views
- Planometric views
- Perspective views

Orthographic projection

Orthographic projection is the name given to the technical, dimensioned drawings that allow a product to be manufactured.

As discussed earlier in this book, you should use third angle projection when producing orthographic drawings.

A rendered pictorial view of the model figure on the right can be produced using orthographic projection.

Component views are dimensioned. Assembled views do not normally show dimensions, unless there are some sizes that are only relevant to the assembly views.

A title block is shown on each sheet containing production drawings to give some information about them.

The orthographic views and a rendered view of the assembled figure are shown here.

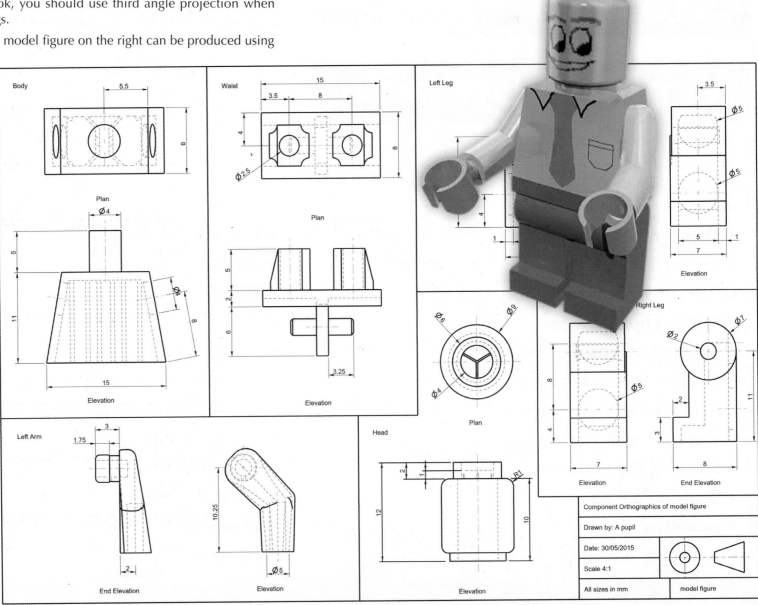

TECHNICAL DRAWINGS

Sectional views

Sectional views are produced to show the internal detail of an object. They cut away part of an object and show what is left. No hidden detail is ever shown in a sectional view.

When a sectional view is made, a cutting plane is used to show where the cut has been made. The part behind the arrows is cut away.

This is a cutting plane.

A cutting plane has a few features:

1. Thicker lines at the ends.

2. Arrows showing the direction of the cut. Everything behind the arrows is removed.

3. Letters to label the cutting plane and sectional view. These are required as more than one cutting plane may be evident.

Hatching lines show where material is cut in a sectional view and should be drawn at 45°. They are drawn in different directions or with different spacing to show different materials or parts.

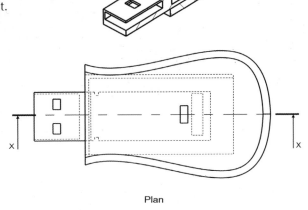

Plan

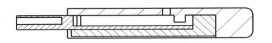

Sectional Elevation on XX

Herringbone

It is important that hatching lines on a sectional view do not meet each other to create a herringbone pattern, as this does not follow British Standards. An example of an incorrect herringbone pattern is shown here.

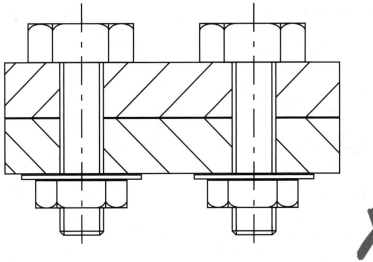

You can see from the drawing below the correct method of hatching two materials.

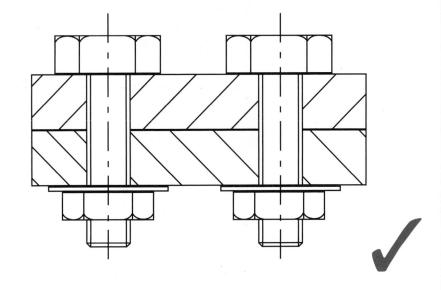

Full sectional views

Full sectional views cut all the way through an object.

The view here is a pictorial view of the model figure with a full section applied. The orthographic views of this are shown next to it.

You can see that the sectional view is labelled as **Sectional End Elevation on AA**. This identifies the view as the sectional view of the cutting plane labelled AA. It still follows the same rules as the third angle projection method, which is why it is referred to as a sectional end elevation.

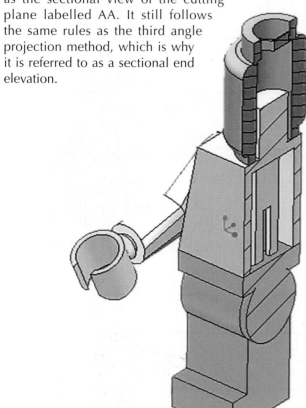

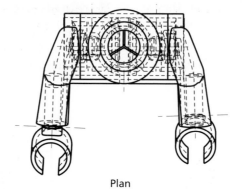

Plan

Cutting plane labelled as AA

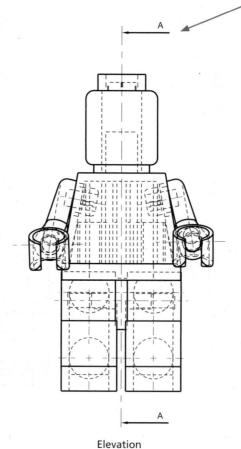

A

Elevation

A

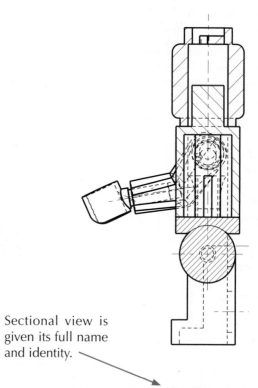

Sectional view is given its full name and identity.

Sectional End Elevation on AA

Half-sectional views

Half-sectional views cut away a quarter of the object. They are given the name 'half-section' as they cut away half of a full section.

Stepped sectional views

Stepped sectionals can also be called offset sections. They allow a cutting plane to change direction.

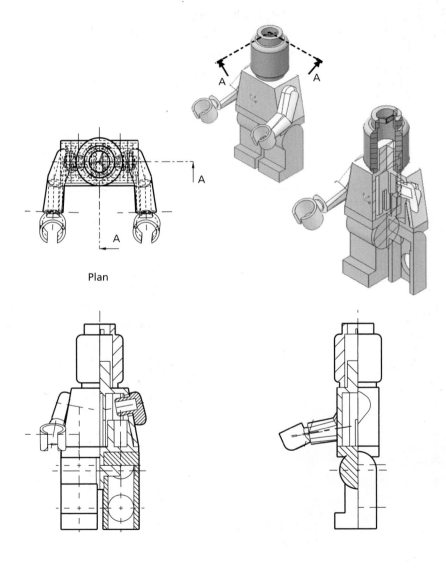

Plan

Sectional elevation on AA

Sectional end elevation on AA

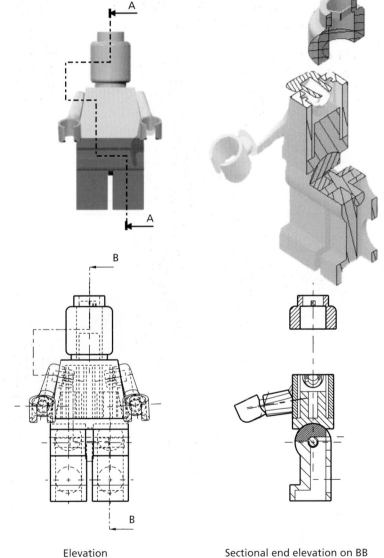

Elevation

Sectional end elevation on BB

Revolved sectional views

Revolved sectional views show the sectional view within the elevation of an object. They are rotated around a centre line and at 90° to it. The sectional view is shown on top of the elevation.

These views are useful to save space and show the section of a long, constant-sectioned object.

Removed sectional views

Removed sectional views are similar to revolved sections, but are drawn outside of the original view. A cutting plane is used to show where the section is made.

They are used to show small details and to help with clear dimensioning where required. For this reason, they are often drawn in enlarged scale.

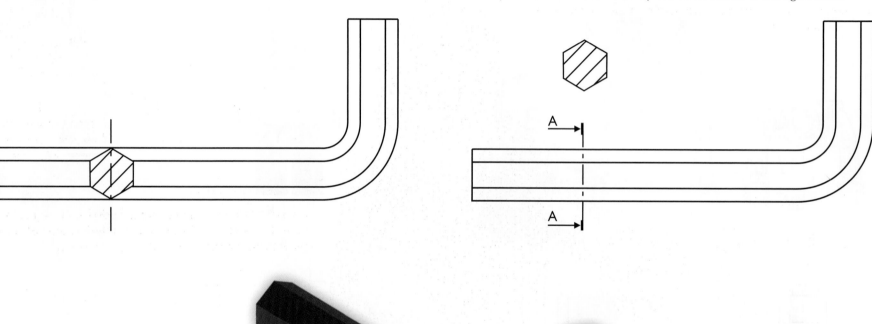

This is a hex Allen key. The elevations of it are shown in the views above.

Part-sectional views

Part-sectional views are used when only a small part of the internal shape of an object is required and a full or half-section may not be needed. You can define the outside of a part-section with a break line or a combination of a break line and a centre line.

The detail view of the part-sectional elevation of the model figure is shown below. A break line has been used to show the extent of the part-section applied.

Showing Flat Surfaces

Flat surfaces are shown using a cross. This is important as without this cross, they can seem to be round.

The flat surface here is shown as a cross on the orthographic view.

Showing a Web

A web is a sloping bit of material added to an object in order to add strength. Webs are not hatched when sectioned to show them separately from the rest of the part.

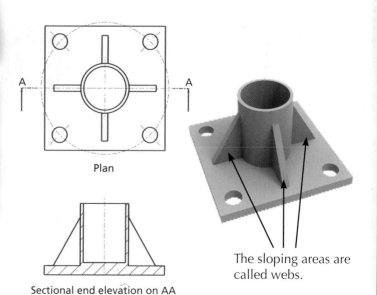

Plan

Sectional end elevation on AA

The sloping areas are called webs.

Isometric views

Isometric views are a type of pictorial view. Specifically, an isometric view is drawn at 30° and 30° angles. They are often used to produce 3D views as they can show a realistic but technically structured view of a product.

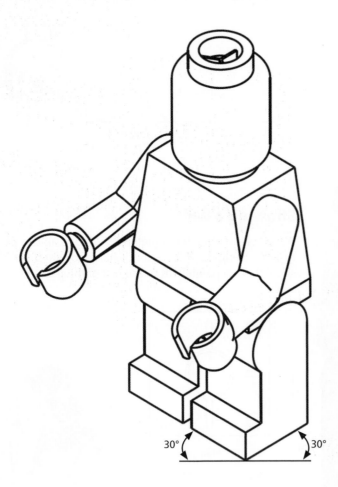

30°   30°

Assembly drawings

Assembly drawings are produced when the various parts of a product are assembled together. As discussed earlier, these are not normally dimensioned but are important to show how an object is assembled.

You need to be able to produce assembly drawings that have a minimum of three parts.

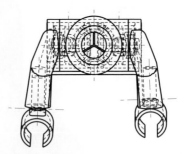

Plan

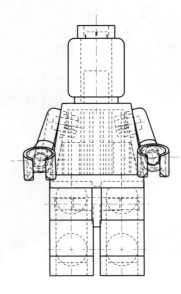

Elevation

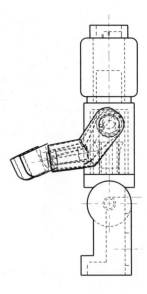

End elevation

Exploded views (full and sectional)

Exploded views allow you to see how a product is assembled. They are often used in flat packs to show people how to build the furniture.

This type of view is included in the production part of a drawing set, as it adds value to the technical detail required to manufacture a product.

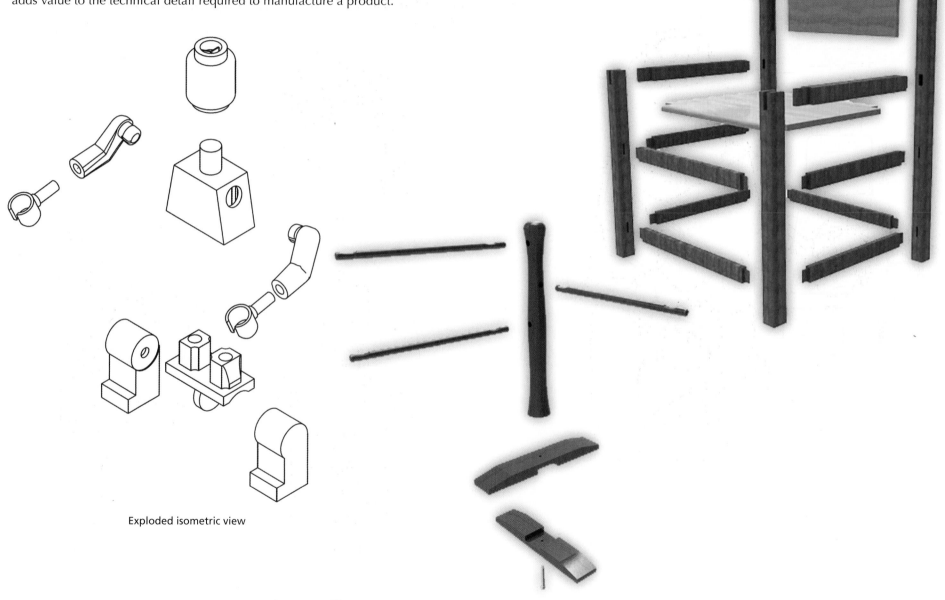

Exploded isometric view

Auxiliary views

An auxiliary view looks at an object from an angle. The rules of projection are still followed but instead of projecting horizontally, like you would for an end elevation, this projection takes place at an angle perpendicular (at right-angles) to an edge on the drawing.

This can be used to show particular parts of a drawing in more detail.

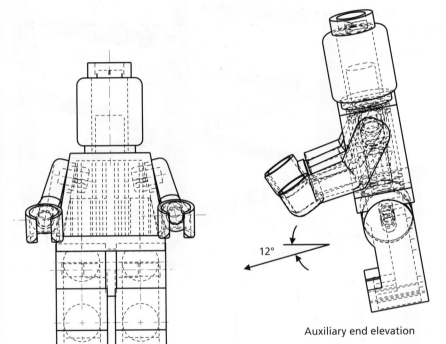

Elevation

Auxiliary end elevation

12°

Ellipses

Ellipses are shapes like squashed circles.

They are dimensioned using the technique shown with the major axis and minor axis.

To construct an ellipse on a computer you use the ellipse tool. On paper, you need to draw two concentric circles, one with the diameter of the minor axis and the other with the diameter of the major axis.

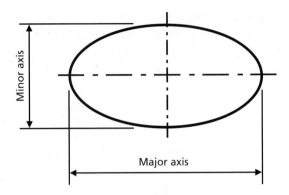

Minor axis

Major axis

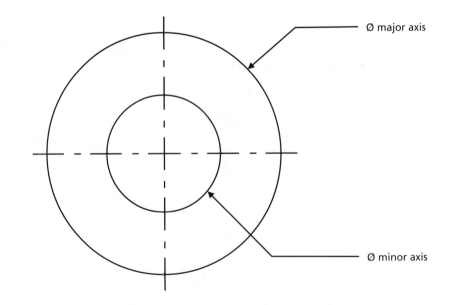

Ø major axis

Ø minor axis

The next stage is to construct a clock face on the circles using lines at 30°.

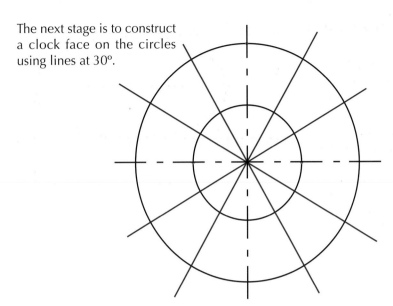

Next, project lines from where the clock face intersects the inner circle vertically outwards.

Mark where these lines cross the horizontal lines with a dot.

You can remember this with the saying:

inside out, outside in.

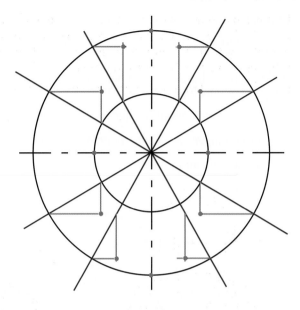

Take horizontal lines from the points where the clock face lines cross the outer circle in towards the centre.

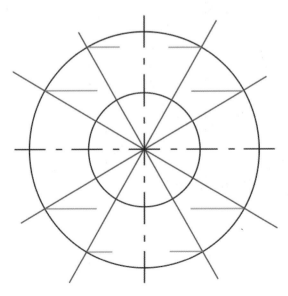

You can draw the ellipse by joining the dots with a smooth freehand curve.

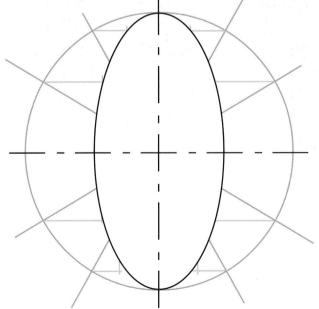

Tangency

Tangency is where a line or curve meets another curve at one point only.

Points of tangency can be found easily when using CAD software using the tangent snap.

When using a drawing board, tangency has to be calculated and found using manual techniques.

You need to know about two types of tangency:

1. Internal tangency – where a circle or arc is inside another.

2. External tangency – where the circles or arcs are outside each other.

Internal and external tangency location

To calculate where to draw an arc or circle that is tangent to another line or curve, you need to know the following two features:

1. Its radius or diameter.

2. The exact point for its centre.

For **internal tangency**, **subtract** the radii of the arcs or circles from each other.

For **external tangency**, **add** the radii together.

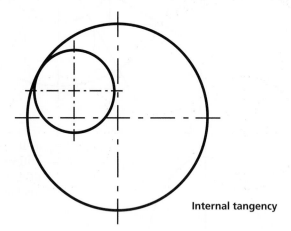

Internal tangency

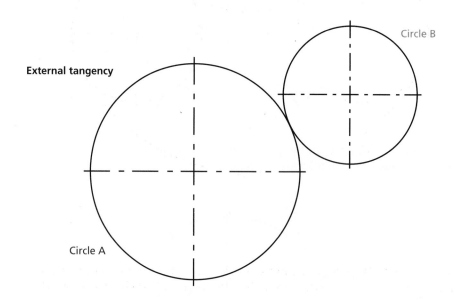

External tangency

Circle B

Circle A

The shape shown here is the base for a gate nameplate. Tangency is used to create the arcs on the top and on the left- and right-hand sides.

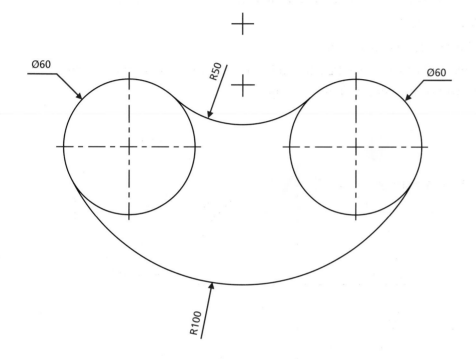

When drawing tangent arcs, you have to identify whether the arcs are inside or outside each other. Remember, if the arcs are outside each other, then add the radii. If the arcs are inside each other, then subtract the radii.

Drawing the first tangent arc

The first stage of drawing the tangent arc on the top of the nameplate is to find the centre of the arc.

The arcs are outside each other, so the radii must be added. With a pair of compasses set to 80 mm (30 mm (half the circle's diameter), plus the 50 mm radius of the tangent arc) draw two arcs, one from the centre of each circle.

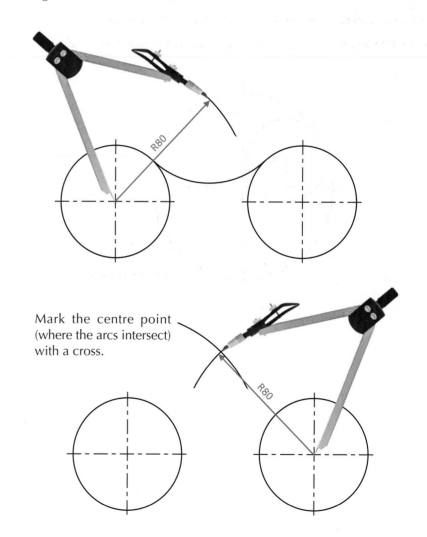

Mark the centre point (where the arcs intersect) with a cross.

The pair of compasses are then set to the correct radius of 50 mm and the tangent arc is drawn from the centre point created.

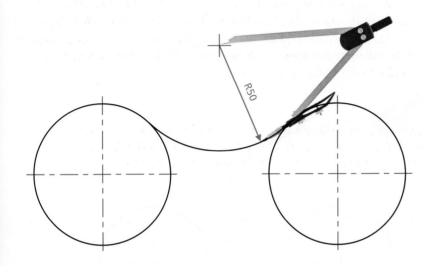

Here the top curve is shown clearly. Notice the centre mark is displayed as a cross to show the centre of the tangent arc.

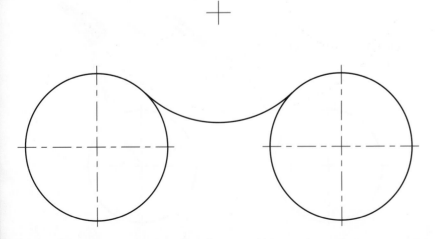

Adding the second tangent arc

Next you need to find the centre of the other tangent arc.

As the two circles will sit inside the arc, the radii must be subtracted from one another. Therefore, the pair of compasses need to be set to:

100 – 30 = 70 mm.

An arc is drawn from the centre of one of the circles.

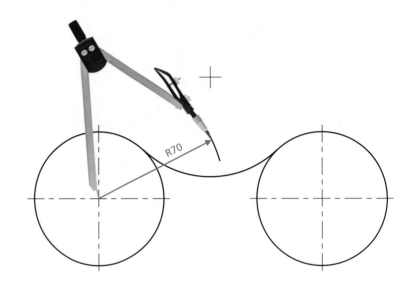

An arc is then drawn from the centre of the other circle. The centre of the tangent arc is at the point where the two arcs intersect.

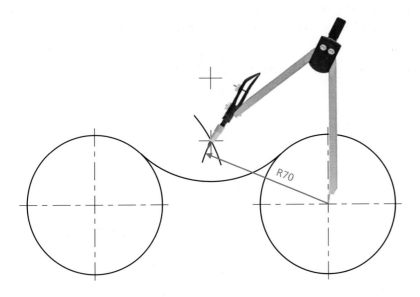

The tangent arc can now be drawn at the correct radius.

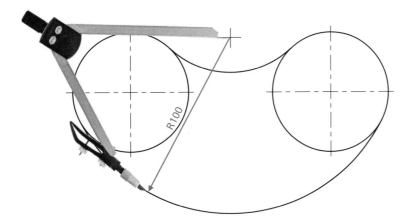

The completed nameplate with the centre marks is shown below. Even though this method was traditionally used on a drawing board, you can use these techniques in a sketch when 3D modelling.

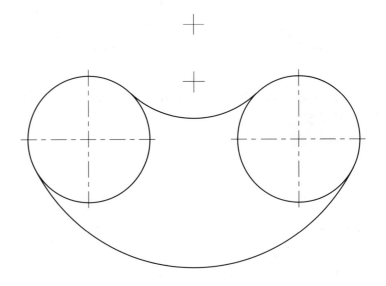

Interpenetration

Interpenetration is the name given to the line where two joined pipes meet.

This is shown on the illustration below.

In 3D modelling software, this is produced by using an angled workplane. However, it is important that you know how to produce a line of interpenetration using manual methods, as you may need to identify the process or select the correct view in your exam.

 Exam Tip

While drawing boards are not used, you can be asked to plot points on a grid so learn this method.

The first stage is to draw a circle on the centre line of the sloping cylinder. This needs to be done on all views.

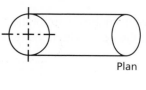
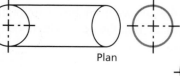

Plan

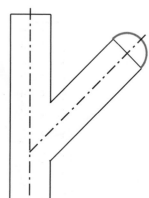
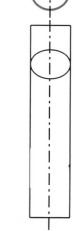

Elevation   End elevation

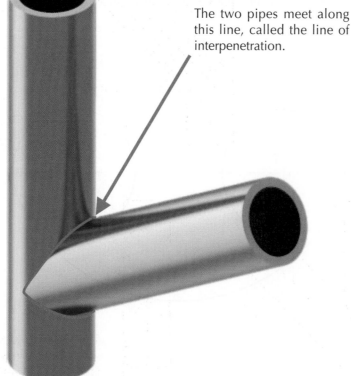

The two pipes meet along this line, called the line of interpenetration.

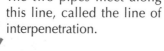

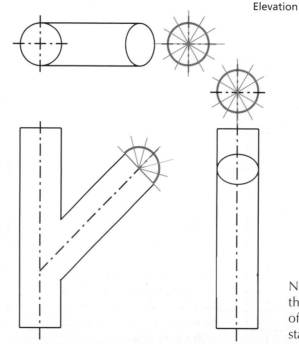

Next create a clock face on the circles with an angle of 30° between each line, starting from the centre line.

Now draw projection lines at the same angle as the pipe in each of the views.

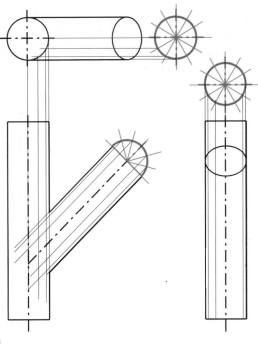

The numbers enable you to find the points for the curve of interpenetration. You have to project horizontally across the views from the number 1 point to the number 1 line. Then, project from the 2 (12) point to the 2 and 12 lines, and so on.

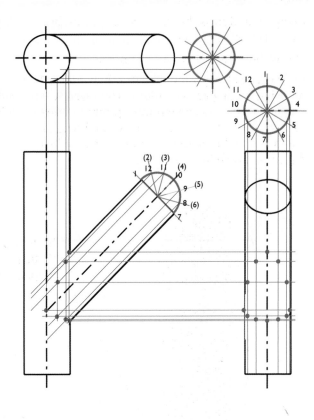

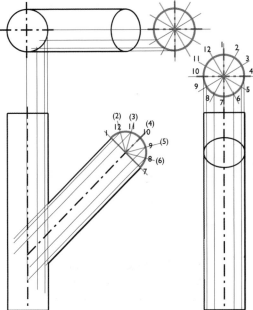

The key stage of the process is to number the clock faces on the two views. These numbers should correspond with each other.

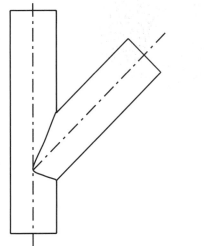

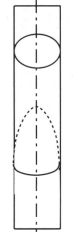

The final stage is to join these dots with a smooth freehand curve. Remember to show hidden detail where required. This completes the line of interpenetration.

Intersections of right prisms and cylinders

Creating intersecting shapes is easy using modern 3D CAD packages. These software packages also generate the orthographic views of the intersecting shapes.

Old fashioned manual methods required the draughtsperson to create these views using a projection line. It was important to accurately number each of the edges of the shapes in order to create these views.

You may be asked to demonstrate your understanding of this process in the exam.

The drawing below shows how the 45° projection line, or bounce line, can be used to generate the lengths of the edges of the prism for the elevation. Third angle orthographic projection works on this basis to create all the parts of the views.

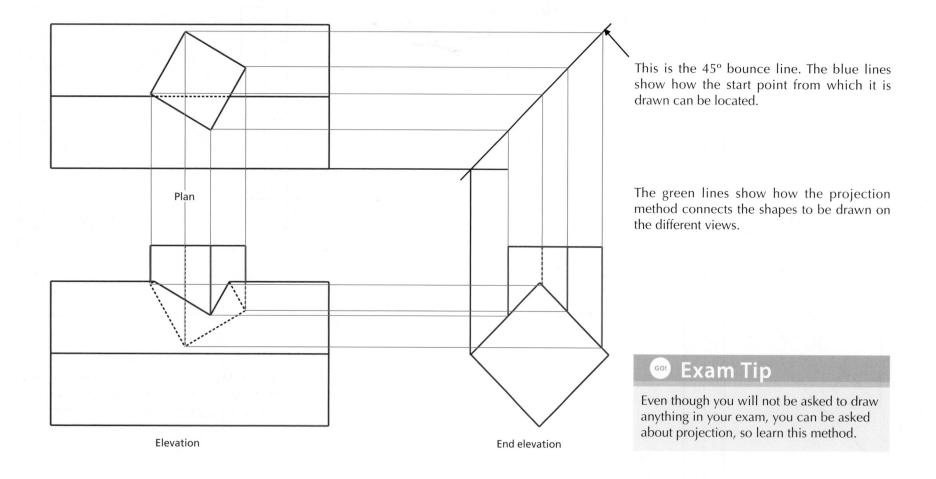

This is the 45° bounce line. The blue lines show how the start point from which it is drawn can be located.

The green lines show how the projection method connects the shapes to be drawn on the different views.

Plan

Elevation

End elevation

GO! Exam Tip

Even though you will not be asked to draw anything in your exam, you can be asked about projection, so learn this method.

TECHNICAL DRAWINGS

It is important to get the position of the bounce line correct. Project the bottom line of the plan horizontally and the left-hand side of the end elevation vertically. The point where the two lines (shown in dark blue) cross is where the 45° bounce line should begin.

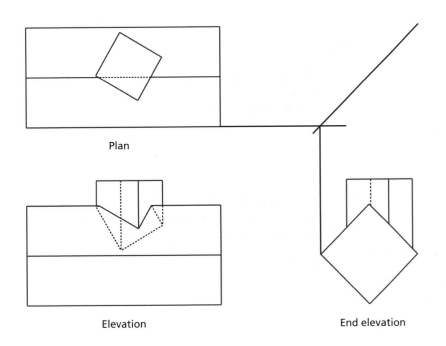

Plan

Elevation

End elevation

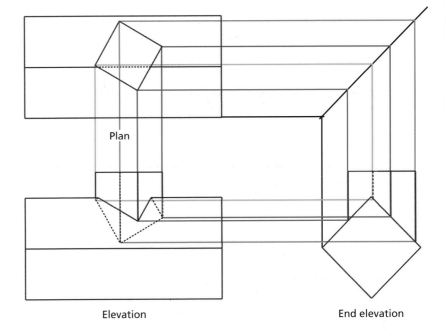

Plan

Elevation

End elevation

You can see from this diagram how the lines correspond with each other to produce the lengths of the edges of the prisms on the elevation.

True length and true shape

True length and true shape are important when talking about the sloping faces of 3D prisms. When looking at these 3D objects in an orthographic view, the viewer cannot see the actual shape of the sloping face. Viewing the face as a true shape allows this.

3D CAD packages will produce these types of views for you within an auxiliary view.

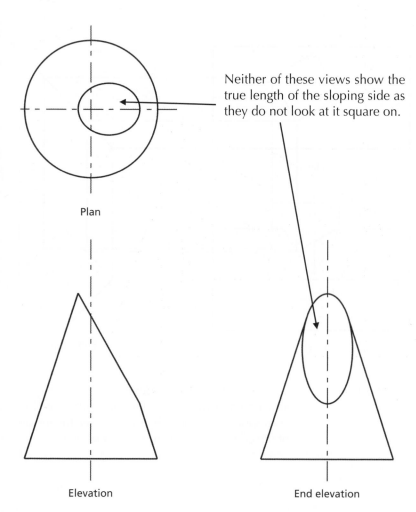

Neither of these views show the true length of the sloping side as they do not look at it square on.

Plan

Elevation

End elevation

Draw horizontal lines across to the elevation from the end elevation. Make sure you draw from the top, centre and bottom of the sloping face.

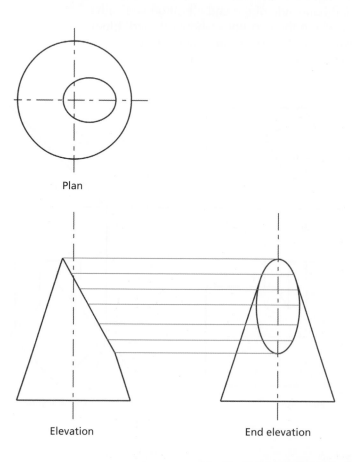

Plan

Elevation

End elevation

> **GO! Exam Tip**
>
> You should understand how to produce true shapes using manual methods so that you can identify the correct view in your exam.

Extend the lines from the elevation at 90° to the sloping edge into the open space above the end elevation.

The next step is to draw a centre line parallel to the sloping edge on the elevation in the space above the end elevation. This is important as the widths from the end elevation will be projected onto this view from this line.

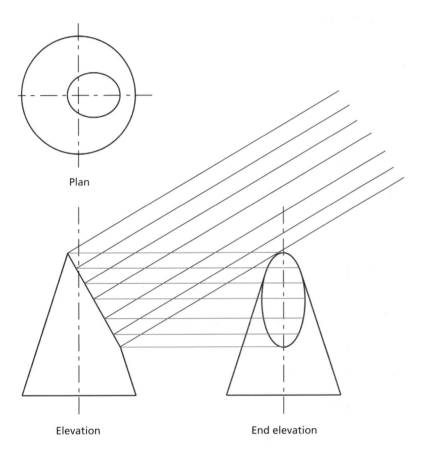

Plan

Elevation   End elevation

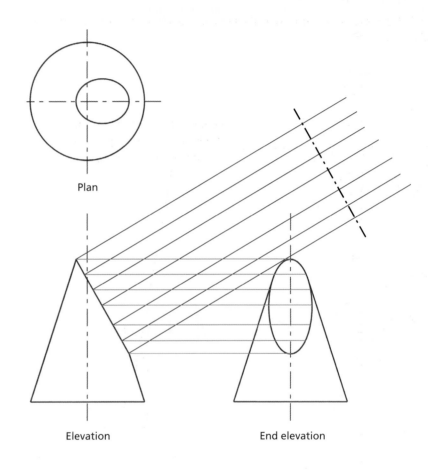

Plan

Elevation   End elevation

Next, use a pair of compasses to project the widths from the end elevation onto the true shape. Make sure you mark both sides of the centre line as shown below. Repeat this for each of the lines.

The top and bottom lines have points on the centre line.

To complete the drawing, draw a smooth freehand curve to join the points.

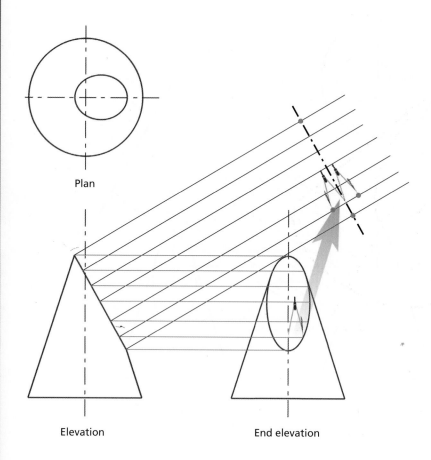

Plan

Elevation

End elevation

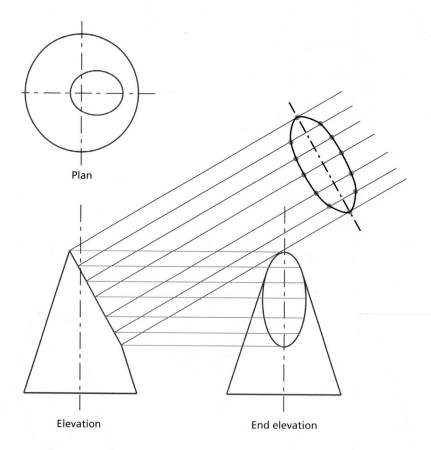

Plan

Elevation

End elevation

TECHNICAL DRAWINGS

Auxiliary views – using CAD

Auxiliary views allow true shapes to be shown in context with the rest of the view of the object.

Using 3D CAD software, auxiliary views can be created at the click of a button. However, you need to know how this is done using manual methods, as you may be asked about it in your exam.

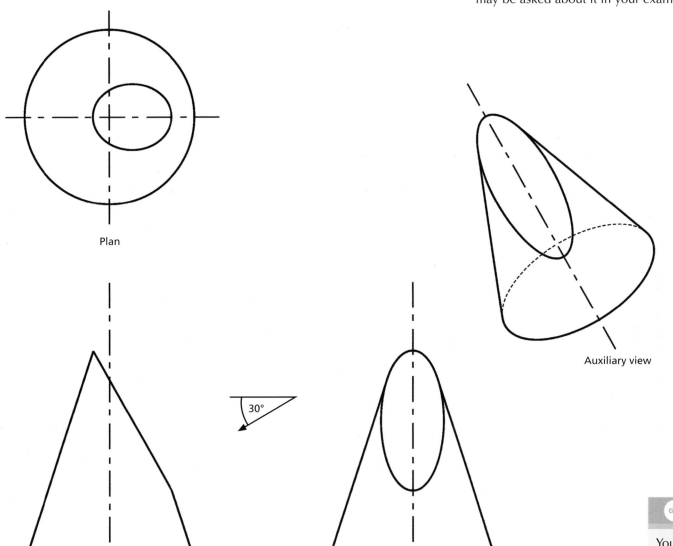

Plan

Elevation

30°

End elevation

Auxiliary view

TECHNICAL DRAWINGS

Auxiliary views can be produced manually using the following method.
Take slices through the object and project these up to the plan.

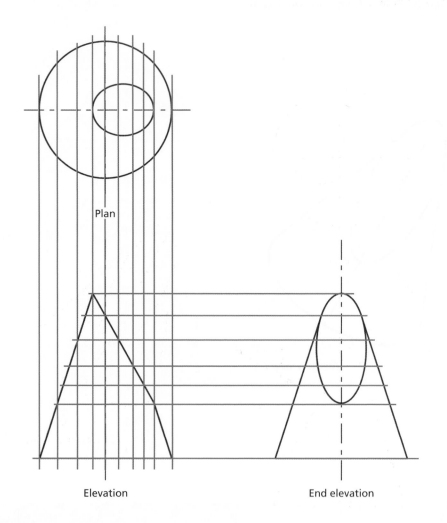

Plan

Elevation

End elevation

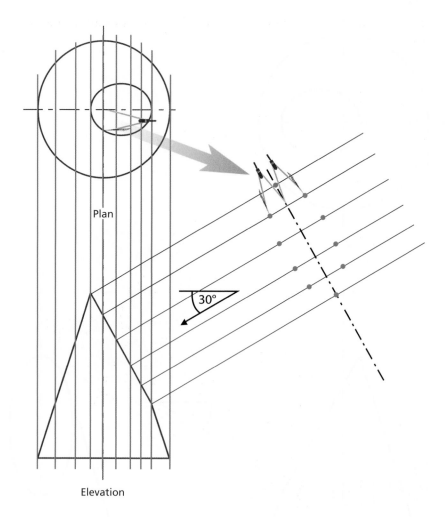

Plan

30°

Elevation

TECHNICAL DRAWINGS

One tip for creating auxiliary views is to complete one surface at a time. This makes it easier to keep track of the points that will be made on the drawing.

Use a pair of compasses to transfer the sizes from the next curve to the auxiliary view.

Finally, add the outside edges to a view. Ensure that any hidden detail is shown. In this example, the part of the curve on the base needs to be shown as hidden detail.

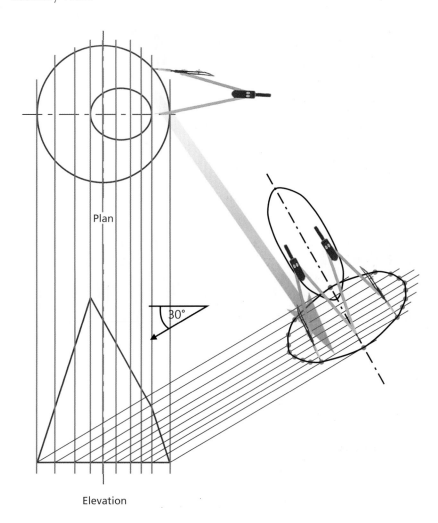

Plan

30°

Elevation

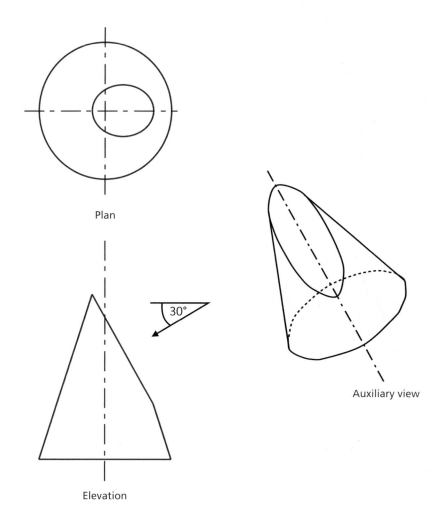

Plan

30°

Elevation

Auxiliary view

Surface development

Surface developments are flat shapes that either fold or roll to make a 3D object. This type of drawing is commonly used for manufacturing in sheet metalwork.

You can use computer software such as Pepakura Designer to produce surface developments from an STL file of a 3D model. *Please note that using the sheet metal function in Autodesk Inventor will not produce accurate drawings so avoid using this method.*

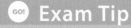

GO! Exam Tip

You need to know how to produce surface developments using manual methods for your exam, as you may be asked to identify the correct surface development for a given view of intersecting shapes.

To produce surface developments manually, first you need to produce orthographic drawings of an object.

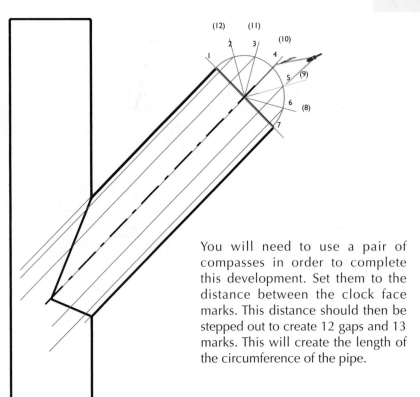

You will need to use a pair of compasses in order to complete this development. Set them to the distance between the clock face marks. This distance should then be stepped out to create 12 gaps and 13 marks. This will create the length of the circumference of the pipe.

This shows the pair of compasses being used to create the 12 spaces for the development.

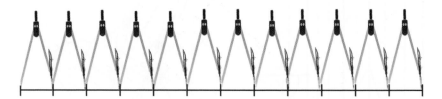

TECHNICAL DRAWINGS

The marks should be extended upwards vertically to complete the next stage of the development.

Number the lines on the grid and use the pair of compasses to mark the lengths of the intersecting pipe onto the grid. Shown is length number 1. You should repeat this for each of the remaining lengths.

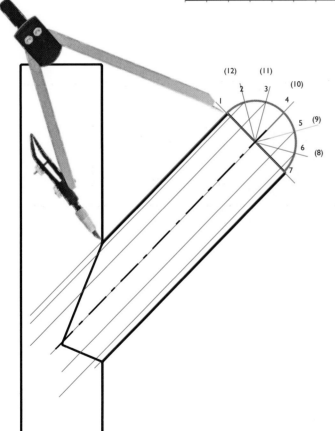

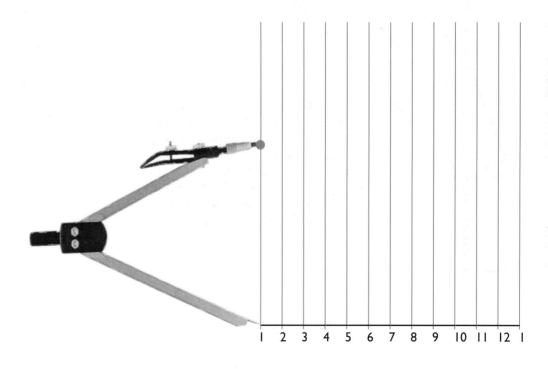

Once all of the lengths have been marked onto the development grid you should see a pattern of marks like the one shown below.

A pair of compasses have been used to transfer all of the lengths from the elevation of the intersecting pipes onto the development.

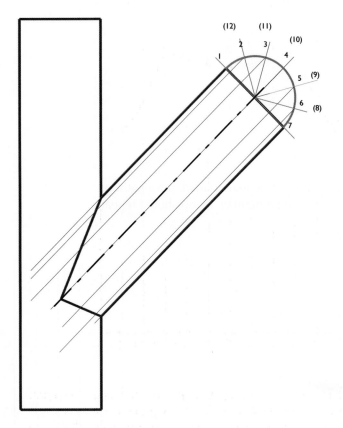

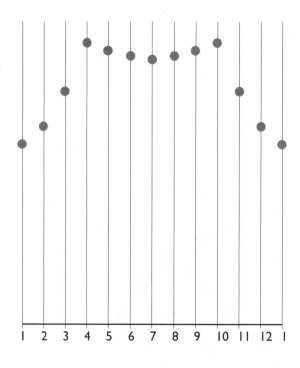

These marks should be connected using smooth, freehand curves.

Ensure that the base and outside edges are outlined to complete the development. This will make the development stand out against the construction lines.

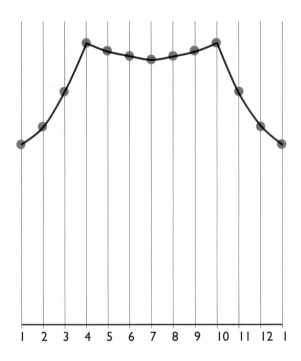

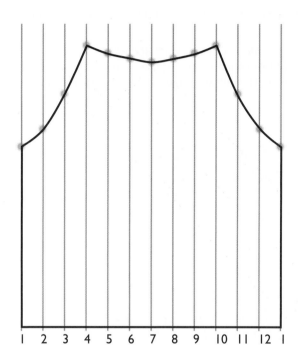

This is the manual method for creating developments of intersecting pipes. You need to have an understanding of this as you may be asked about it in the exam. You can see why it is far easier to use computer software to create these automatically from 3D CAD models and why such software is used in modern industry.

Oblique views

Oblique views are the most simplistic pictorial drawings that can be produced. An object is drawn from the front, like an elevation. The depths are then projected or sketched back at 45°. In a cabinet oblique drawing, the depths are drawn at half the full size. A cavalier oblique drawing is used when it is preferable to show the depths drawn full size.

The advantage of using oblique drawings is that circles can be shown accurately and clearly from square on and the shape of the circle is not distorted in any way. This allows engineering components to be shown clearly.

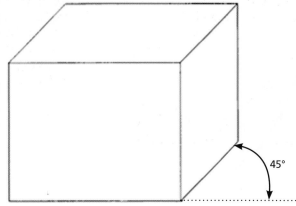

45°

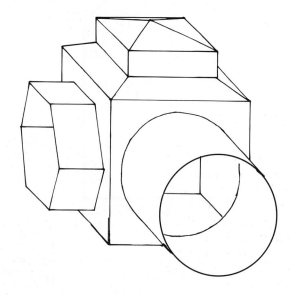

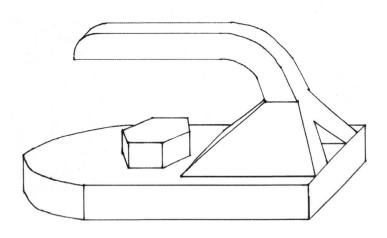

Planometric views

Planometric views are commonly used by interior designers. Due to the angles they are drawn at, they can clearly display the internal details of a room. Planometrics are either drawn at 45° and 45° or 30° and 60°.

Rendered CAD drawings like the one shown here are often used to show room layouts. They are produced in perspective rather than a strict planometric format to make them appear more realistic. However, their purpose (showing the interior layout of buildings) is the same.

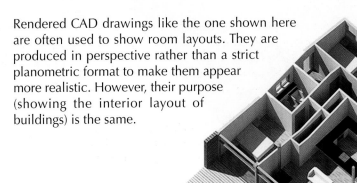

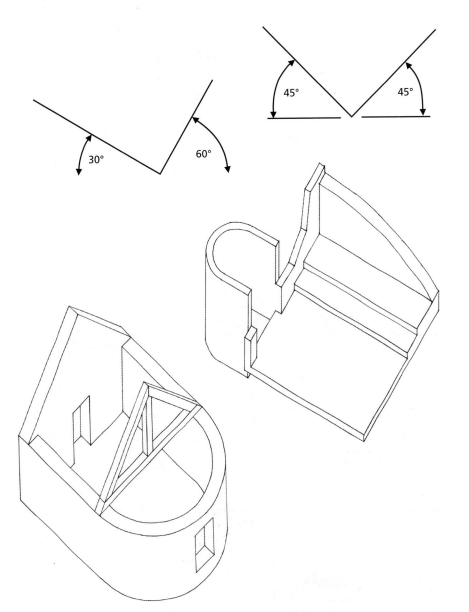

Perspective views

Perspective views is a realistic method of sketching where lengths appear to get smaller the further away from the viewer they are. Lines are taken to vanishing points in order to produce the perspective effect. You will produce one-point and two-point perspective sketches when producing preliminary drawings during the Higher Graphic Communication course. It is also likely that the CAD rendered environments you produce will be shown in perspective to give the most realistic views for promotional graphics.

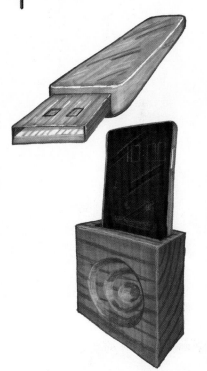

Chapter 5

Creating Promotional Layouts

You will learn

- The colour wheel
- Design elements and principles
- Grid structure
- DTP features – an overview

The colour wheel

Colour is the most important choice for you to make. The colour wheel is used to plan colour schemes for promotional graphics.

It quickly shows how colours will harmonise or contrast with each other.

Primary colours

The primary colours are red, blue and yellow.

Secondary colours

The secondary colours are violet, green and orange.

Tertiary colours

Tertiary colours are mixes of primary and secondary colours.

Contrasting colours

Contrasting colours are on opposite sides of the colour wheel. They can be used together to create impact and can be eye-catching.

Harmonising colours

Harmonising colours are next to each other on the colour wheel. They can be used to create a soft or gentle feel.

GO! Assignment Advice

It is easy to take the colour wheel for granted. This is one of your most useful tools as a graphic designer. Consider it whenever you are developing a layout.

Warm colours

Warm colours are used to give a feeling of warmth to a drawing. They can also be used to show that something is hot as part of a symbol, like a red dot on a hot water tap.

Red	Yellow	Orange

Cool colours

Cool colours are used to give a feeling of coolness to a drawing. They can also be used to show that something is cold as part of a symbol, like a blue dot on a cold water tap.

Blue	Green	Violet

Advancing colours

Advancing colours appear to come towards you when you look at them. They are often used to create impact.

Advancing colours tend to be warm colours:

Red	Yellow	Orange

Receding colours

Receding colours appear to move into the background when you look at them. They are often used as flashbars as they will make an object placed on top of them appear to come forward.

Receding colours tend to be cool colours:

Blue	Green	Violet

Accent colours

An accent colour is a colour used throughout a presentation to help bring it all together. A common mistake is to use too many colours in a presentation. Using one or two colours repeatedly can help to bring all the elements together and create unity.

GO! Assignment Advice

When you are evaluating the various versions of your planned layout during your assignment, refer to the headings relating to colour theory. This will help to meet the assessment requirements for DTP development work.

Design elements and principles

When planning layouts for promotional graphics, there are some guidelines to follow to help produce high-quality presentations.

These can be split into two groups:

- design elements
- design principles

Design elements

- line
- shape
- texture
- size
- colour
- mass/weight

Design principles

- alignment
- balance
- contrast
- depth
- dominance
- unity/proximity
- white space
- proportion
- rhythm
- emphasis
- grid structure

By using these elements and principles and applying them with skill, you can create exciting and impactful presentations for your promotional graphics.

 Exam Tip

List the design elements and principles in the extra space at the end of your exam paper as soon as you begin. There will be a question about them and referring to each of them in turn will help you to write your answer.

Line

You can use line to create many different effects. Some common uses of line include organising parts of a layout, separating parts of a layout or suggesting movement within a layout.

Line can be changed by using different types, styles and colours. Curved or wavy lines can be used to suggest movement or create interest.

The cover of the dice design project shown below uses line to underline text, separate the text on the page from images, act as a flashbar to bring images forward and act as a visual border for the cover. The curved lines create movement through the different dice shown and help bring them forwards towards the reader.

Shape

There are lots of shapes used in presentations. Commonly these will include squares, circles, triangles and polygons like hexagons or octagons.

Squares and rectangles surround us in life so tend to be trusted. They can be seen as boring, but can be made more interesting by rotating them and placing them on top of each other.

Circles and ellipses are used to show a number of different feelings. They are protective, as they suggest a safe region, and they can also be used to suggest movement. As these shapes have no beginning or end point, they can be used to infer reliability and are often used in symbols for car manufacturers for this reason.

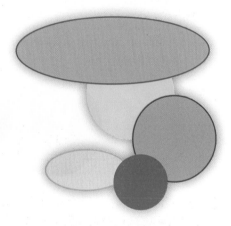

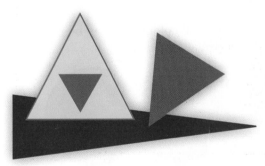

Triangles tend to suggest movement. They can be used to communicate conflict in a presentation due to their sharp corners. They can also be used to show strength and create impact.

Texture

Texture affects the physical feel of the paper used. In product brochures, high-quality paper is used to imply that the product is high quality too.

Texture can also be created by the images on the paper. Old paper can be mimicked using images. Other materials can be represented through the fill options in your DTP software.

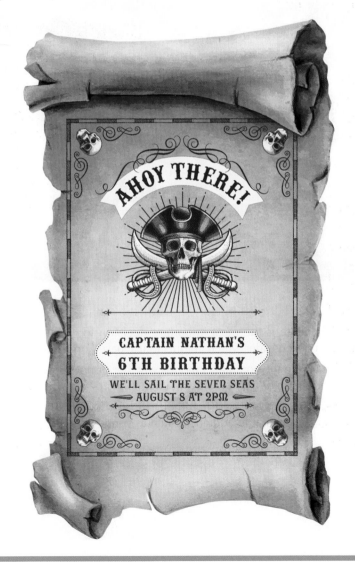

Size

Size can be used in a number of ways. When designing a presentation, you must consider the size of the paper used and how you use the size of fonts and images to highlight the most important elements of the presentation.

Larger objects will be the first things that people notice about your presentation.

Colour

The colour palette is the most important decision to make when designing a DTP layout. You must consider which colours to use based on a number of different factors.

These will include the company colours, whether or not you want to convey emotion, present information or appeal to a particular market.

Primary colours can be used together to create contrast and target a product or presentation at a particular audience, such as young children.

Warm colours

Yellow, orange and red are considered warm colours and can create a feeling of aggression, excitement or danger. These colours appear to advance from the page.

Cool colours

Blue, green and violet are cool, calming colours. They are also receding colours and can be used for flashbars, to help an object stand out from the page.

Neutral colours

Brown, black, white and grey are neutral colours and can be used to create formal, natural or simple presentations.

Mass/weight

Mass refers to the size of an element or the amount of space it occupies. The mass of an object can be increased by giving it dark colours or by making it larger in size.

When choosing text styles, their mass and weight should be considered. Chunky fonts will add mass to an area of the presentation, while smaller-structured fonts can be used to help balance a promotional item.

Mass and weight are commonly used in relation to other items on the page to create rhythm.

Alignment

There are four main types of alignment:

1. Left alignment

2. Right alignment

3. Fully justified

4. Centred

Alignment should be used to maintain rhythm in a presentation. It can be used to clearly show which sections of text go together and which belong to an image.

Left alignment	Right alignment	Fully justified	Centred
———	———	———	———
———	———	———	———
———	———	———	———
———	———	———	———
———	———	———	———

Balance

Balance can be either symmetrical or asymmetrical. This is like thinking of the page as a set of scales. A heavy object can be balanced by smaller objects positioned further away from it and lighter objects can be balanced by darker objects (darker objects appear to have more weight than lighter ones).

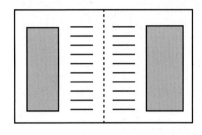 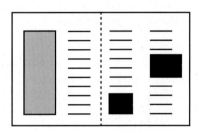

Contrast

Contrast is where opposites are used in some design features for effect. This could be shape, text, colour, line or weight.

A word in a *contrasting font*, colour or size makes it **stand out**.

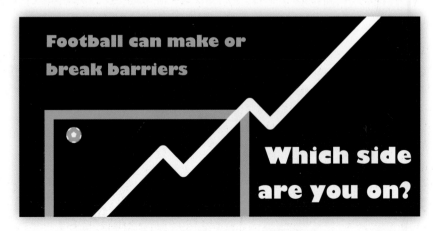

Football can make or break barriers

Which side are you on?

Depth

A presentation can be given a sense of depth by arranging the elements in front or behind each other. This can make some parts of the DTP presentation appear to come towards the viewer.

In the example below the object being advertised is placed in front of both a wavy line and a gradient fill flashbar. This combination of DTP features makes the image appear to come forward. This effect is further enhanced by the use of a drop shadow.

Dominance

Dominance refers to how you can make particular parts of the presentation stand out. It means that the presentation is read in a particular order due to the relative size of the elements within it. This is known as the hierarchy of the layout.

In the example below the product being advertised is the most dominant element, then the woman wearing headphones and then, finally, the text describing the product. Visually directing the order, or hierarchy, in which the poster is read helps the viewer to quickly understand what the product is.

Unity/proximity

Unity can be created in a presentation through repetition of shape, images with a common theme, repetition of font styles and the positioning of different parts in relation to one another. Positioning parts close together shows that they belong together, e.g. an image and its caption are kept close together to show they are related.

The advertisement below uses red and white throughout to make it clear that all the elements belong together. The repetition of curves in the lines and subheading also creates unity, as does the proximity of the text to the image of the woman.

White space

White space is the areas on a page that are left blank. This can be used to help balance a presentation or to focus the reader's attention on the content of the presentation. White space is vitally important to prevent a presentation from being too busy or cluttered.

The blank areas on the advertisement below ensure that the viewer focuses on the images and text without any distractions.

Proportion

Proportion is all about the relationship between elements on a presentation. Large images will dominate a layout and can communicate to the reader what it is about before they even start to read the text.

On the advertisement on page 90, the images account for half the area of the advert. This effective use of proportion graphically emphasises the topic of the advert. The title is clear and helps to link the two images.

Grid structures can help you to incorporate proportion. When designing a grid structure for a longer publication, like a magazine or a book, it can be good to use different proportions on either side of a spread (two facing pages). This prevents the pages from looking too boring or regimented. You can see how the left and right margins of the facing pages in the master page for this book are reversed in order to give better proportions across the two-page spread. This also helps to create a nice rhythm, as the reader is guided from the outside to the centre of the book.

Larger margin on the outside of the page than inside for good proportions.

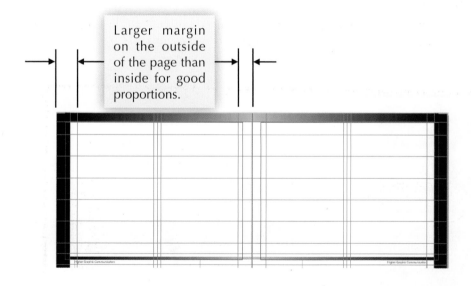

Rhythm

Rhythm is used to create movement through a presentation. This can be achieved by repeating elements and using shapes to infer movement. Various parts of a presentation can be connected with lines, shapes or colours.

The use of triangles here gives the business card rhythm by creating movement from the top left corner to the bottom right corner. The repeated use of golf balls also creates rhythm by leading the reader along the top and bottom of the card toward the contact details.

Emphasis

You can place emphasis on particular parts of a presentation by using various techniques. Bold text can be used to make particular words or parts of a presentation stand out. Text along a path can be used to contrast with other more regular shapes in a presentation. Drop shadows can give emphasis to both images and text. Bold and reverse text can also be used to make a particular feature stand out from the presentation.

Some features of a presentation can be used as a focal point in order to attract attention and quickly convey the subject of the presentation.

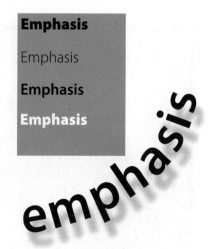

Grid structure

rule of thirds

The rule of thirds is a guide, inspired by the golden ratio, that is used by photographers. Imagine a grid that splits a page into three equal segments both horizontally and vertically and place the main parts of the presentation on these grids lines. Some cameras have this function installed on them to assist with layout.

Here is a picture of Edinburgh Castle. You can see how it has been split up using a rule of thirds grid to help the balance of the picture.

Headphones Tidy

Life is too short to tangle

The rule of thirds can be used as a basis for grid structures to help lay out DTP presentations or to inform asymmetrical grid structures.

GO! Assignment Advice

When you evaluate the planned layout for your assignment, ensure that you use the terms covered in this section in your annotations. You need to comment on the role they play in your DTP presentation to meet the assessment requirements.

Symmetrical grid structure

Symmetrical grid structures are the same on both sides of a layout. They are formal and used when order is important and the layout needs to be highly organised.

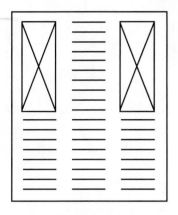 

Asymmetrical grid structure

In an asymmetrical grid structure, the two sides of a page or double-page spread are different. Using this type of grid structure can create impact and interest and make something look modern or appeal to young people.

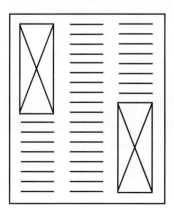 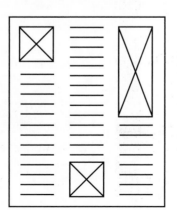

Choosing a grid

Often designers will explore different methods of structuring a layout by quickly sketching some ideas. However, the majority of the development of the layout will be completed using DTP software. This gives the advantage of being able to use real images, the various DTP features and the quality of production that using computer software offers over hand-produced methods. It also speeds up the development process.

You can see how the designer has developed the structure of the layouts below using DTP software. Each has been developed through stages using images and all of the DTP features.

DTP features – an overview

Look at the layout on the right. We will describe how the design elements and design principles have been used to produce this layout.

Proportion – The image is the largest element on the page. The reader will notice this first, so it creates a hierarchy in the layout. The title is the next thing to be noticed, as it is the second largest item, which leads the reader to the main part of the magazine article.

Line – This is used to help organise the text at the bottom left-hand side of the layout. The lines guide the reader down the columns of text containing the examples of types of tree.

Line is also used as a column rule to help separate the columns of text on the facing page, so it is easier to read.

Balance – The mass of the left-hand side of the page helps to balance the busy right-hand side of the page where most of the information in the article is located.

Alignment – The text 'Types of Trees' is left aligned with the line that the hardwoods are listed alongside.

The text on the right-hand side of the page is all right aligned to create structure and a clear relationship between all of the elements.

Texture – The texture of the tree bark and leaves in the image contrasts with the smooth background underneath the image, which has been used to make the text easier to read and stand out from the image.

Size – The ever-decreasing sizes of text direct the reader from the main heading to the subheadings and then on to the extended body text.

TYPES OF TREES

Hardwoods

Beech – a very hard, straight-grained wood, which can survive in harsh conditions.

Mahogany – a reddish-brown wood often used to make expensive furniture.

Oak – a very hard wood, which requires a high level of skill when working with it.

Teak – this wood is highly resistant to outdoor conditions, making it ideal for garden furniture.

Softwoods

Scots pine – this wood contains lots of knots, but is easy to work with.

Spruce – although not particularly durable, this wood is often used for fence panelling.

Yellow cedar – this is a pale yellow, light wood, which can be quite stable.

European redwood – this is a cheap wood with lots of knots. However, once a protective finish is applied it is quite durable.

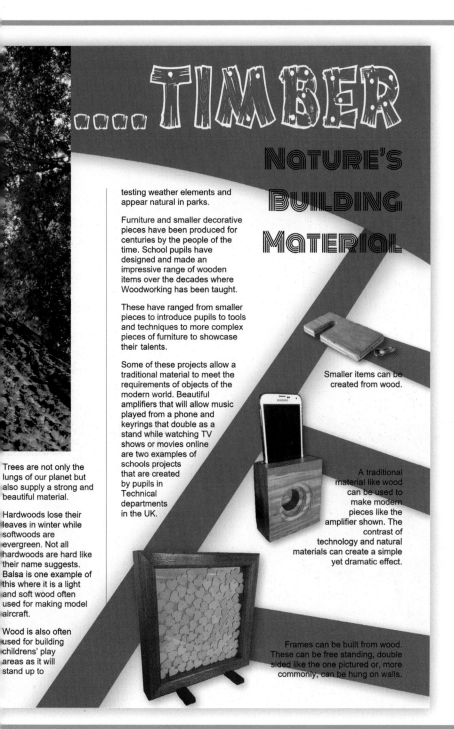

TIMBER

Nature's Building Material

testing weather elements and appear natural in parks.

Furniture and smaller decorative pieces have been produced for centuries by the people of the time. School pupils have designed and made an impressive range of wooden items over the decades where Woodworking has been taught.

These have ranged from smaller pieces to introduce pupils to tools and techniques to more complex pieces of furniture to showcase their talents.

Some of these projects allow a traditional material to meet the requirements of objects of the modern world. Beautiful amplifiers that will allow music played from a phone and keyrings that double as a stand while watching TV shows or movies online are two examples of schools projects that are created by pupils in Technical departments in the UK.

Trees are not only the lungs of our planet but also supply a strong and beautiful material.

Hardwoods lose their leaves in winter while softwoods are evergreen. Not all hardwoods are hard like their name suggests. Balsa is one example of this where it is a light and soft wood often used for making model aircraft.

Wood is also often used for building childrens' play areas as it will stand up to

Smaller items can be created from wood.

A traditional material like wood can be used to make modern pieces like the amplifier shown. The contrast of technology and natural materials can create a simple yet dramatic effect.

Frames can be built from wood. These can be free standing, double sided like the one pictured or, more commonly, can be hung on walls.

Colour – Green is used throughout the layout to reinforce that trees are a natural resource.

Rhythm – The repeated squares leading into the heading 'Timber' lead the reader from the large image to the main article.

Shape – The green, sloping shape is used to direct the reader down the page, through the various parts of the layout. The branches off the main shape reflect the structure of a tree, reinforcing the topic of the article.

Emphasis – Drop shadows have been added to the titles on the left page, the images of the products and the background shapes to make them stand out from the page.

Proximity – The images of the products are positioned close to the descriptions to make it obvious that they belong together.

Contrast – The heading and subheading contrast so that they can be easily distinguished from each other. This makes the different parts of the article easier to read.

The images are placed on green shapes that act as flashbars to help them stand out. Additionally, the drop shadows on both the shapes and images help them to stand out from the background.

White space – There is some white space between the main image and the column of text to create some breathing room (an area where the reader's eye isn't distracted by lots of information). There is also space between the images of the wooden products, which creates an invisible boundary between each of them.

Unity – Green is used throughout the article to help bring all the elements together.

Chapter 6

3D CAD Modelling

You will learn

- Drawing tools in 3D CAD
- 3D CAD features and edits
- Using a revolve
- Using the loft tool
- Extrusion along a path
- Using a swept blend
- Types of helix
- Creating a helix
- Intersecting features
- Applying a shell
- Applying a fillet to an edge

- Applying a chamfer to an edge
- The mirror edit
- Using the array tool
- Constraints
- Assembling parts of a model
- Offset
- Tangency
- Assembly files
- Sub-assembly
- Stock or library components – CAD libraries

- 3D CAD views
- 3D CAD rendering techniques
- Terms involved in 3D modelling
- Modelling concepts
- Modelling tree/hierarchy
- Modelling plan
- CAD file types
- CAD libraries
- Online CAD libraries

Drawing tools in 3D CAD

When creating 3D CAD models, you have to use sketches (2D drawings made in the software, from which the models are created). To do this, you will need to use the drawing tools within the software to produce different shapes. Some of these are similar to those used in programs like Word, so it is likely that you will be familiar with them already.

Line tool

The line tool allows straight lines to be drawn.

_____

Circle tool

The circle tool allows you to produce circles.

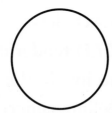

Rectangle tool

The rectangle tool allows rectangles or squares to be drawn.

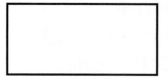

Ellipse tool

Ellipses can be drawn using the ellipse tool.

Trim tool

Unnecessary lines can be removed from a sketch. These lines may have been included to assist with creating the sketch, but can be removed once their use has passed.

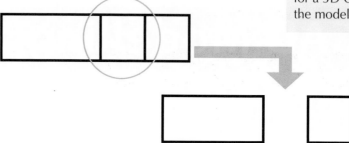

Mirror tool

The mirror tool allows the user to create a mirror image of a shape.

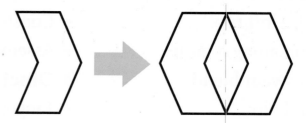

Layers in CAD

When using layers in CAD it is similar to drawing the different details of a drawing on tracing paper. You can draw different details of a drawing on separate sheets within the CAD package. These sheets are called layers. They can be viewed independently or together depending on what the person reading the drawings needs to see. For example, the electrical wiring can be drawn on one layer and viewed separately from the plumbing fittings which can be drawn on a different layer.

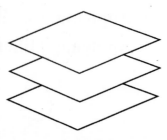

Arrays (linear, box and radial)

The array tool allows you to repeat the same shape in a pattern. This saves time, as you do not need to redraw shapes. A linear array repeats the shape in a straight line, a box array repeats it in two directions and a radial array repeats it in a circular pattern.

Linear array

Box array

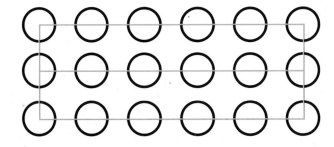

Radial array

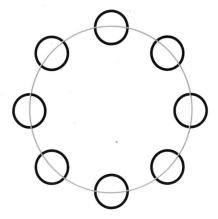

Offset tool

The offset tool will create a line, curve or shape a specified distance from another line or the edge of a shape.

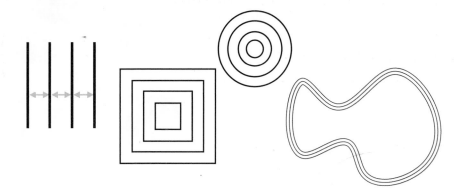

Project edge tool

The project edge function allows you to take a length, or chain of lengths, from a solid and copy (or project) it onto the sketch. This is very useful when it is important to repeat the lengths from a solid on a sketch. This tool is often used in top-down modelling (see page 122).

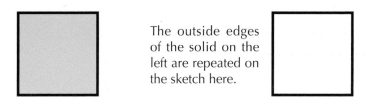

The outside edges of the solid on the left are repeated on the sketch here.

Extend tool

Lines can be extended from sketches to meet the beginning of another sketch. Here, the line is extended across to close the gap in the shape.

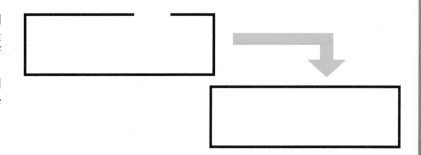

3D CAD features and edits

Creating an extrusion

Extrusions are the backbone of most 3D CAD models. They are the most simple CAD feature available. They create a solid by dragging a shape along a straight line, either up or down, right or left, or forward or back.

The die shown here was created using a number of different extrusions.

You can do three things when extruding shapes:

1. Add material to create solid objects.

2. Subtract material from solid objects.

3. Intersect other solids.

Step 1

To create a cube, like the die shown, a profile of a square needs to be drawn as a sketch.

The sketch of the square will look like this.

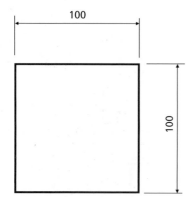

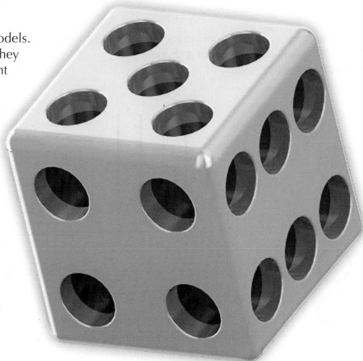

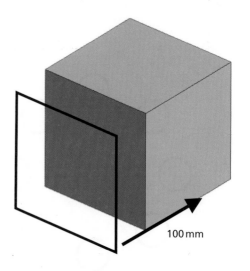

GO! **Exam Tip**

When describing an extrusion, use the following terms:

Step 1: Sketch a **profile**.

Step 2: **Extrude** to a distance.

Use the term **subtract** if removing material from a solid. Show the dimensions used for the profile using sketches. This will make it easier to understand than describing this using words.

Step 2

The square is then extruded to create a solid shape. In this case, the extrude was set to the size required to make a cube.

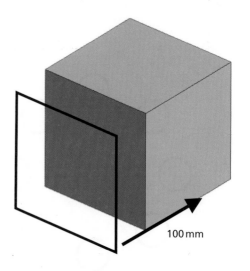

100 mm

3D CAD MODELLING

Subtracting an extrusion

When you remove material from a solid, you must describe this as a subtraction. The numbers on the die are all subtracted from the solid. This is done using the extrude tool with the subtract setting switched on.

Extrude, revolve, extrude along a path, loft and helix can all be used to create a solid and can be switched to subtract from a solid model.

The circular profile for the dot is sketched first.

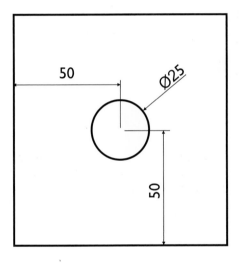

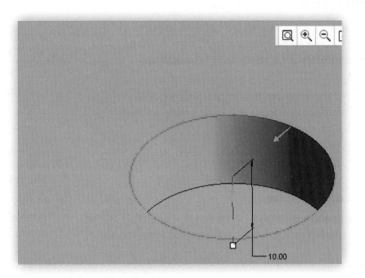

The depth of the extrusion must be specified.

You must also state that you are subtracting material.

GO! Exam Tip

Using software-specific terms like 'remove material' will not gain you any marks in the exam, even if they correctly describe this process. To describe the process of removing material from a 3D CAD solid, you must use the term 'subtraction' to be awarded the marks available.

Once completed it will look like this.

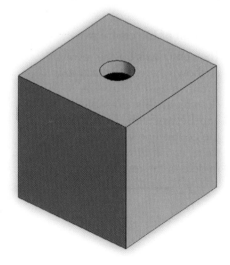

Using a revolve

The revolve feature allows a sketch to be rotated around a centre axis and a solid shape to be created from this. A shape must have rotational symmetry for a revolve to be suitable.

The first stage is to create a sketch with a centre line. The centre line is the centre axis for the revolve. It is important to position the sketch at the correct distance from the centre line for the revolve to be created to the correct dimensions.

Step 1

The profile of the revolve

The profile is the cross section of the revolve. This is the part that is rotated around the centre axis to form the solid.

Step 2

Position of the centre axis

The centre axis for the revolve is shown here. A centre axis is drawn as a centre line in a sketch. In this example, the gap between the sketch and the centre line will mean that there is a hollow part in the middle of the revolve.

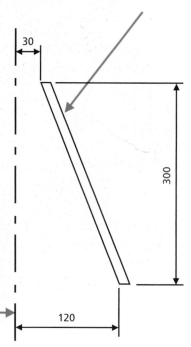

Step 3

Creating the solid

The solid that is created from the sketch is shown here. You can see the revolve was taken around a full 360° and the profile is highlighted in green.

The revolve angle

In this revolve, the profile was taken around 360°.

The profile

The profile is shown in green.

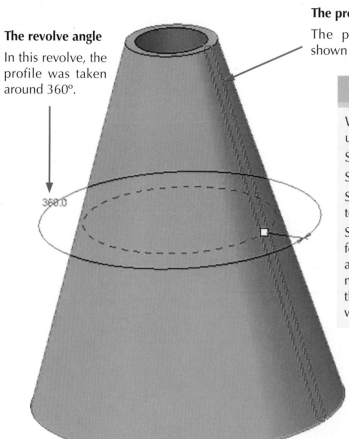

🔵 Exam Tip

When describing a revolve, use the following terms:

Step 1: Sketch a **profile**.

Step 2: Define a **centre axis**.

Step 3: **Revolve** the profile to the required angle.

Show the dimensions used for the profile and centre axis using sketches. This will make it easier to understand than describing this using words.

The revolve tool

The revolve tool can be used to create many different shapes. Just remember that the solid must have rotational symmetry.

If the cross section is irregular then the solid will have to be produced through a revolve rather than through extrusion.

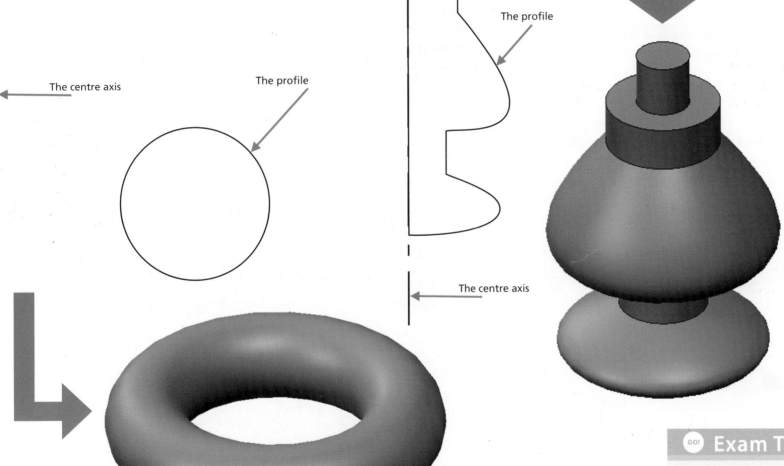

The profile

The profile

The centre axis

The profile

The centre axis

🔘 Exam Tip

The position of the centre axis relative to the profile is very important when producing a revolve, so make sure you define this clearly in your modelling plan.

Using the loft tool

The loft feature allows a range of shapes with different cross sections to be joined together. This can be done with the sections sketched on parallel planes, like the example shown here, or along a path.

Some 3D modelling packages refer to a loft as a 'blend' and approach the command differently. However, it is very important that you refer to this command as a loft in the exam and follow the process for a loft in your answer. It is the only answer or description that will be accepted by the SQA in an exam as correct.

An example of a solid created through lofting is shown here. The three sketches that have been used to create the loft are highlighted in pink in the solid.

Step 1

Creating workplanes

To begin, you must create workplanes for each of the profiles of the loft.

In this case, three workplanes need to be created with the required distance between them.

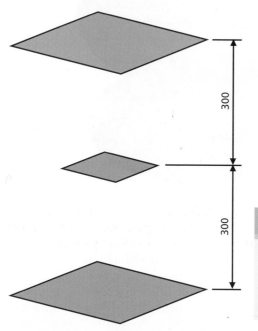

Step 2

Sketching the profiles

The three profiles now need to be sketched. You must show the dimensions used for these profiles.

Previous sketches are shown lighter in Profile 2 and Profile 3 for clarity. You need to show where any new sketch is positioned relative to previous sketches.

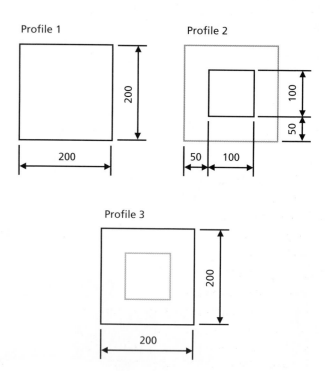

> ### 🚦 Exam Tip
>
> You must use the term **loft** in your exam to describe this feature. Any other commands used by software packages that describe the same process will not be accepted as correct answers.

Step 3

Creating the solid

Now use the loft tool and select the three sketches to create the solid. Define the loft path as straight.

Creating a loft path for a twist

If a loft has a twist in it, like the one shown here, you need to define a path that the loft should follow.

You can show this path by drawing a line from one of the corners of each of the three sketches.

You must clearly show the path that a loft follows in a modelling plan and in any exam answers you give.

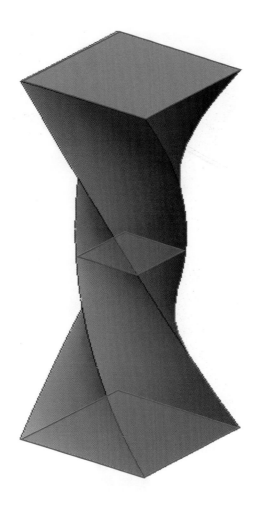

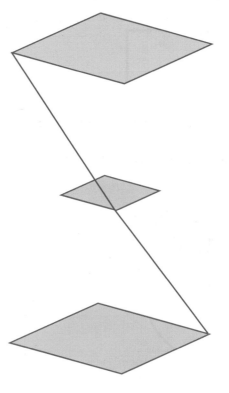

GO! Exam Tip

When describing a loft, use the following terms:

Step 1: Create **workplanes**.

Step 2: Sketch **profiles of each**.

Step 3: Define a **loft path**.

Step 4: Use the **loft** feature to create the loft.

Show the dimensions used for the workplanes and profile using sketches. This will make it easier to understand than describing this using words.

The path is shown here in green. You can see how the path moves along one corner at a time as it moves up through the three profiles.

Extrusion along a path

The extrude along a path (or sweep along a path) tool allows the user to form a solid along a sketched path.

The teapot handle shown here was created by extruding along a path.

Step 1

The profile of the extrude needs to be sketched.

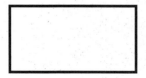

Step 2

The path the extrude along a path will follow must be sketched.

Step 3

The extrude tool can then be used to create the solid.

The solid shown in yellow was created by the profile following the path.

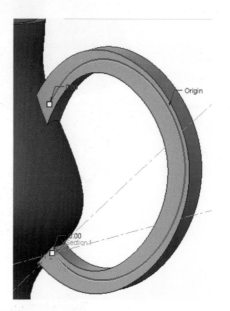

GO! Exam Tip

Some 3D modelling packages simply refer to this as a sweep. If you are asked to describe this feature in your exam, you must call it **sweep along a path** or **extrude along a path** to be awarded the mark.

GO! Exam Tip

When describing an extrusion along a path, use the following terms:

Step 1: Sketch a **profile**.

Step 2: Define a **path**.

Step 3: **Extrude the profile along the path.**

Show the dimensions used for the profile and the path using sketches. This will make it easier to understand than describing this using words.

Using a swept blend

A swept blend is a combination of lofting and extrusion along a path. It allows the solid to have different cross sections along the path, as shown here in the teapot spout.

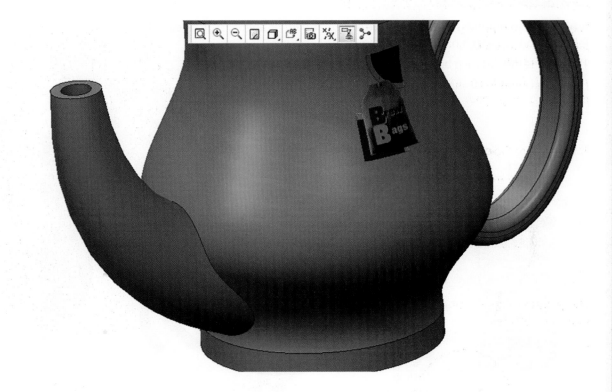

The teapot spout is created by first sketching a path, then sketching a cross section at one end of the path and a second, different cross section at the other end of the path.

The small circle at the top of the spout is the first section of the swept blend.

The large circle at the base of the teapot is the second section of the swept blend.

The path of the swept blend is shown here.

Exam Tip

This command will not be included in your Higher exam. It has only been included in this guide to help you with more advanced coursework.

3D CAD MODELLING

Types of helix

A helix is a spring-like solid. It can have a regular path or angled path. It can also follow a constant pitch or a varied pitch.

The pitch is the distance between each of the points on the curve.

Examples of helix are shown here.

A helix can be created with a taper. This can be done by changing the taper angle.

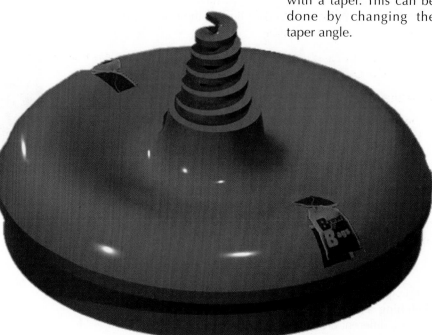

Pen springs often have a varied pitch. This can be modelled using a helix and changing the settings to allow this.

Car springs tend to be larger in size and are more likely to use a constant pitch.

3D CAD MODELLING

Creating a helix

You must follow these steps when creating a helix:

1. Sketch the centre axis for the helix.

2. Create the profile of the helix.

3. Set the size of the pitch. (This is the distance between the points on the individual coils of the helix.)

4. Define whether the helix is clockwise or anticlockwise.

5. Define the length of the helix or the number of revolutions you would like it to have.

Steps 1 and 2

Create the centre axis and the profile for the helix. The centre axis will be defined as a centre line in the sketch. The profile will be a closed shape. You must define the dimensions of the profile and its distance from the centre axis (the offset distance).

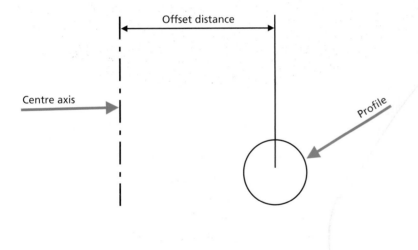

Step 3

Set the pitch of the helix. The pitch is the distance between the individual turns. The pitch cannot be made smaller than the height of the profile.

The pitch is the distance between the points on the individual coils of the helix.

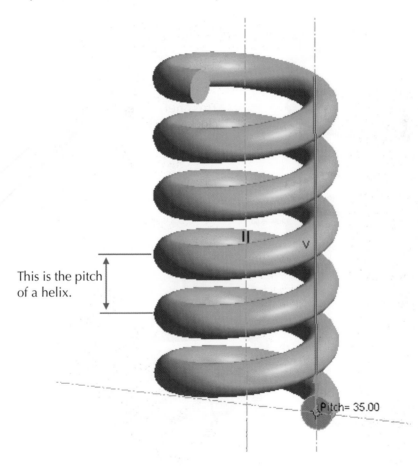

This is the pitch of a helix.

Pitch= 35.00

Step 4

A helix can be either clockwise or anticlockwise.
Make sure you choose the type you require.

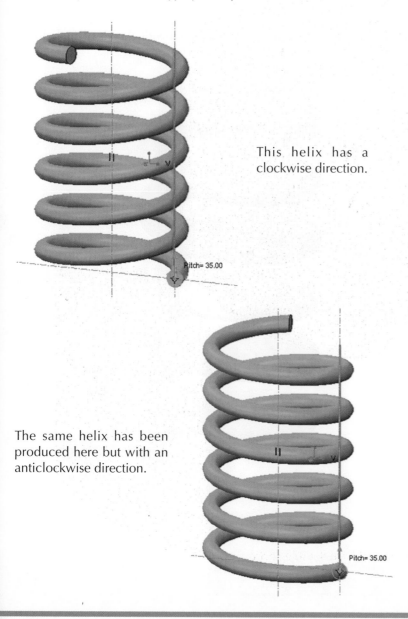

This helix has a clockwise direction.

The same helix has been produced here but with an anticlockwise direction.

Step 5

Finally, either set the length of the helix or define the number of turns the helix has.

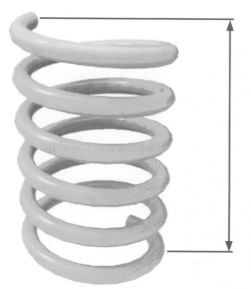

The length of this helix has been set to 200 mm.

With the combination of the length and the pitch used in this example, you can see how the helix starts and ends on different planes. You may have to take this into consideration when creating a helix.

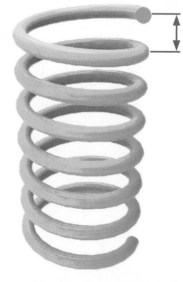

This is one turn. You can see how there are seven turns for this helix.

This version of a helix has seven turns. Notice how the helix starts and ends on exactly the same plane.

Intersecting features

It is possible to create a solid from the overlapping parts of two solids.

Here two square blocks have been extruded. The area of intersection is the square formed at the point where the two blocks cross. This has been highlighted to make this clearer.

Another example is when two elliptical solids are intersected.

This solid is then produced.

This solid is created from the intersection.

Applying a shell

The shell tool is used to hollow a solid object and create a constant wall thickness. The user must specify the wall thickness they require.

You can select one or more faces of the solid to open up and project the shell through.

GO! Exam Tip

When describing a shell:

Step 1: State that you will use the **shell** command.

Step 2: Specify the **wall thickness**.

Step 3: If you are opening an end of the solid, identify which faces this applies to.

Applying a fillet to an edge

A fillet will round off an edge on a solid.

You can set the radius of the fillet to whatever size you need. This radius can be constant or elliptical.

The edges of the teapot handle have been rounded off using a fillet.

 **Exam Tip**

When describing a fillet:

Step 1: State that you will use the **fillet** command.

Step 2: Specify the **radius**.

Step 3: Select the edges you will fillet.

Applying a chamfer to an edge

A chamfer will add an angle to an edge on a solid.

You can set the size of the chamfer to whatever you need.

You can see that a chamfer has been applied to the outside edge of the wooden box shown here.

The chamfer tool is selected and the size of the chamfer is set by the user. The edges are selected and then the chamfer is created.

 **Exam Tip**

When describing a chamfer:

Step 1: State that you will use the **chamfer** command.

Step 2: Specify the **size** and **angle**.

Step 3: Select the edges you will chamfer.

The mirror edit

The mirror edit allows a component to be created with a mirror image applied to a defined workplane or face. In the example shown here, a company that manufactures brass nameplates starts with a half shape and then mirrors it to create a symmetrical shape. This allows the company to adjust the overall length of the shape for names of different length whilst maintaining symmetry.

You can see that the face on the thin side has been selected as the mirror plane.

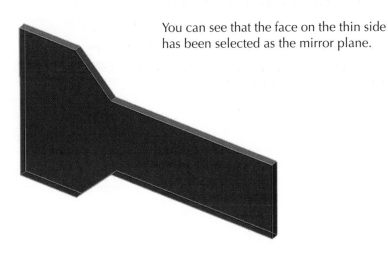

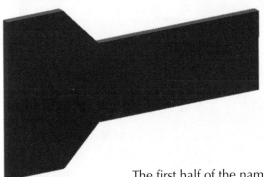

The first half of the nameplate is shown here.

The original half of the 3D model is repeated on the other side of the selected mirror plane.

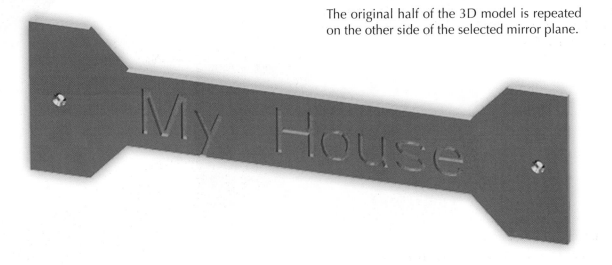

Using the array tool

The array tool is used to repeat a feature in a pattern. These patterns can be arranged in different ways. Most commonly they are arranged along a straight line, in a box or in a circular pattern.

Radial array

To create a radial array of a 3D modelled feature, you need to set an axis in the centre of the circle. The feature will already have been created. In this example, the hole is to be repeated in a circle around the base of the teapot.

GO! Exam Tip

State you are using a **radial array**.

Step 1: Define the **centre axis** of the array.

Step 2: Set the **angle** between the repeated feature.

Step 3: State **how many repetitions** you will create.

There are commonly two settings used to specify how the array should be completed: the number of times the feature is to be repeated and the required angle between each feature. Often, the position of the repeated features will be represented by a dot before the settings are accepted. This allows the user to check their work before completing the array.

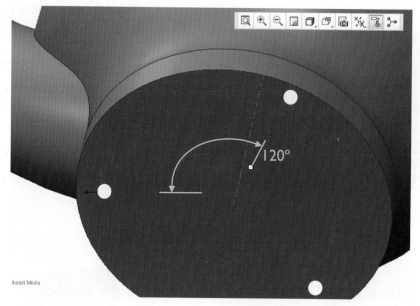

The axis is placed in the centre of the radial array.

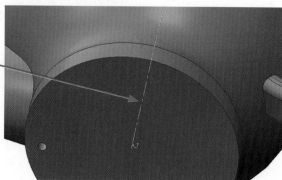

The feature can be applied once the required settings are entered.

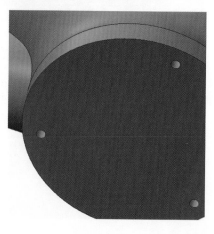

Linear array

A linear array allows a feature to be repeated along a straight line with a set distance between the repetitions.

In the pencil holder shown here, the holes for the pencils need to be repeated to make five holes along the top of the aluminium bar.

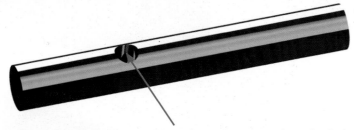

First, the feature needs to be selected, which in this example is the hole. Then the direction of the array needs to be defined.

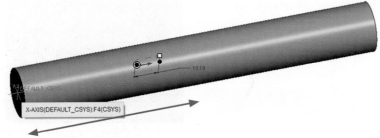

The direction is shown by the coordinate system display.

The number of features and the distance between each of the repeated features needs to be set.

This example has five features with a distance of 20 mm between each of them.

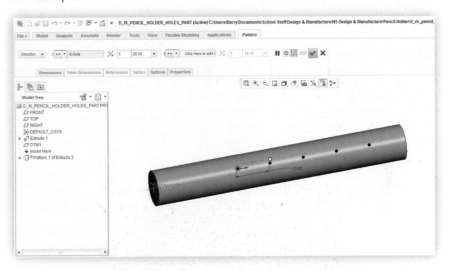

Exam Tip

State that you are using a **linear** array:

Step 1: Define the **direction** of the array.

Step 2: Set the **dimension between the repeated feature**.

Box array

A box array allows a feature to be repeated along the *x*-axis and the *y*-axis in the pattern of a box.

This key holder shows the results of a box array.

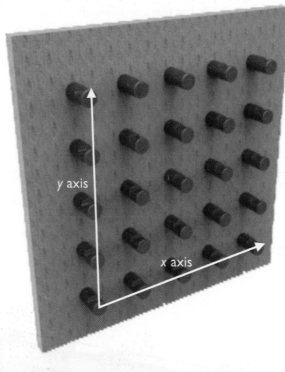

The original feature is one peg created at the bottom corner of the board.

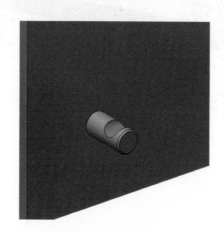

Once the feature has been selected then the array can be set. The two directions are set by selecting edges of the solid. Then the settings for the distance between each repetition and the number of repetitions are entered.

Often the software will show a preview of where each feature will be repeated using dots.

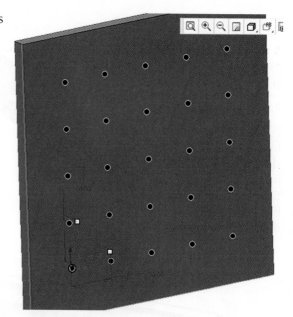

In this example, the box array is completed once the pegs are created in the pattern required.

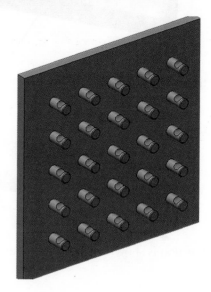

Curve array

A curve array will repeat a 3D form along a curved path. This is very useful for creating fencing.

The first step is to create the solid form. In this case a cylinder has been created for fence posts.

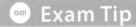 **Exam Tip**

You will not be asked about this type of array in your exam. It is included in this book to help you create more advanced models.

Next a curve for the path of the array has to be sketched.

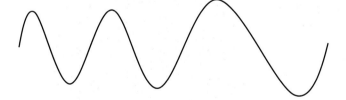

The parameters for the curve array are entered into the option boxes.

The array will be previewed on the screen. The positions of the solids will likely be represented by black spots.

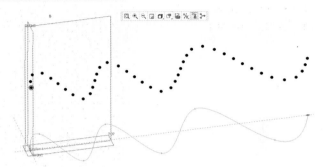

The completed curve array is shown here.

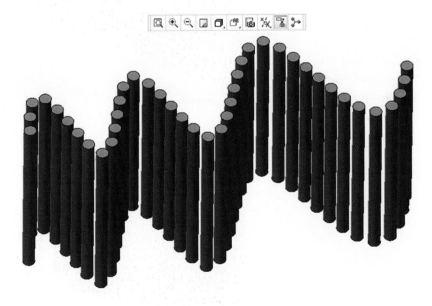

Constraints

Constraints are helpful drawing tools that can assist the production of CAD models by giving some feedback on the types of line or shape being sketched.

Linear

A linear constraint will lock a straight line to a vertical or horizontal direction. Usually a small H or V is used to signify the lines as being horizontal or vertical.

It can also be used to help the user draw lines along the same horizontal or vertical plane.

This is often shown by small lines on the sketch.

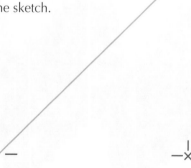

Perpendicular

A perpendicular constraint will lock a line at right-angles to another line. This is often indicated by a symbol on the sketch.

Radius or diameter

This constraint allows the radii or diameters of circles in a sketch to be locked at a specific size. This is useful where a number of circles of the same size are required, as only one needs to be dimensioned.

R

Parallel

A parallel constraint will lock lines in parallel to one another. This is useful, especially when drawing angled lines.

This constraint is shown by two small angled lines beside each of the straight lines being drawn.

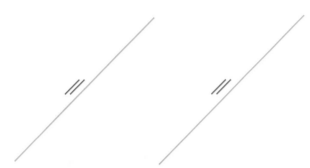

Tangent

A tangent constraint will snap a circle or straight line to the tangent point of another circle.

This is often shown by a T.

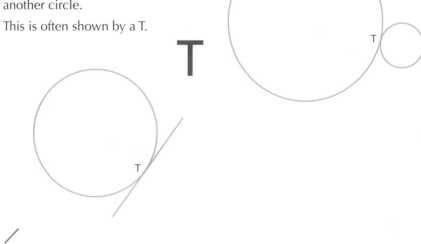

Concentric

A concentric constraint will help to draw circles with the same centre. The cursor will snap to the centre of a previously drawn circle to ensure accuracy.

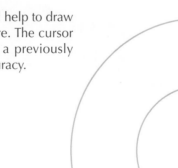

 Assignment Advice

Using these constraints will help you produce accurate 3D CAD models when working on your assignment. Develop your knowledge of them during your coursework.

3D CAD MODELLING

Assembling parts of a model

When creating 3D models of objects, we create the different components as separate files and then assemble them to build up complete products.

This has many advantages:

- It allows more realistic models to be created.
- It allows moving parts to be animated.
- It allows exploded views of the object to be easily created.

The pen shown here has been assembled from its component parts.

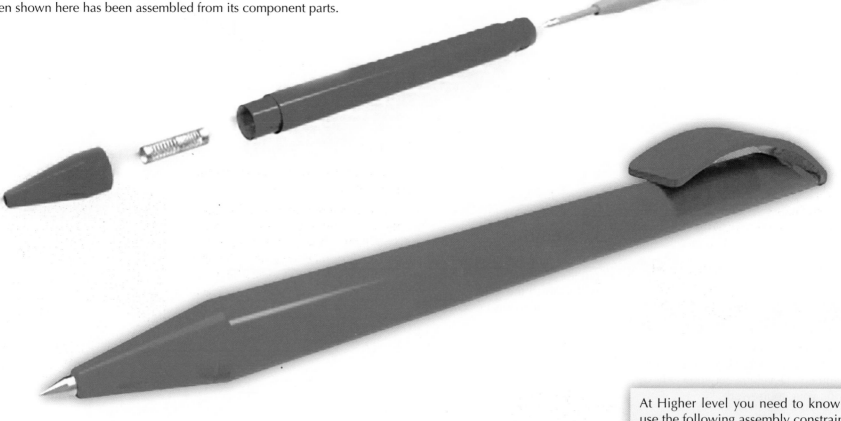

The methods of assembling the different parts are called constraints. These constraints define the relationship between the parts.

At Higher level you need to know how to use the following assembly constraints:

- centre axis/centre align
- mate
- align
- offset
- tangent

Centre axis/centre align

When aligning circular objects, the centre align tool can be used. This will make all the round surfaces line up. It is very useful when you are looking to insert a round bar into a round hole.

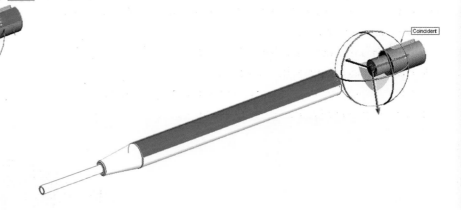

Mate

The mate tool makes faces touch each other.

Here the ink stopper for the pen is to be lined up with the inkwell. The two flat surfaces that are to touch each other are assembled. They are selected and then mated to achieve this.

Align

The align tool places faces on the same plane.

You can see the difference between the mate and align command here. The same two faces that were selected to mate the objects (on the left of the page) are selected here.

The align has set the faces on the same plane, rather than lined up to meet each other.

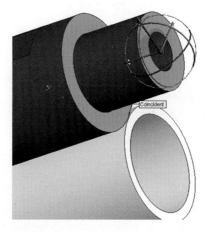

Offset

The offset tool allows the user to set faces at required distances from each other.

Here the desk has been set to be a specific distance from the edge of the room. The side of the desk and the side of the room are selected in the same way they would be for either a mate or align assembly, but the distance at which they are to be placed is entered.

The two faces here have been selected and an offset has been applied between them.

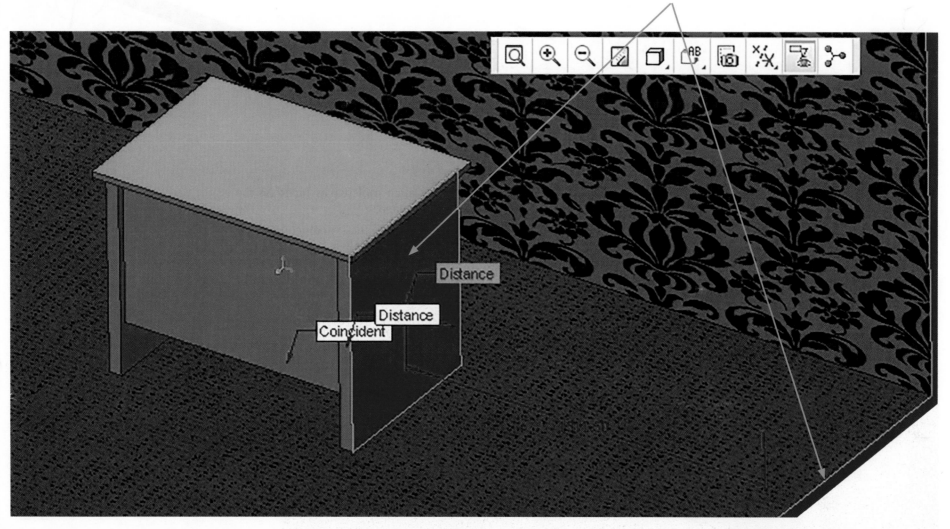

Tangency

The tangency tool allows the user to set curved faces to touch each other at one point only. You can see in the example of the pencil holder here how the curved faces of the tubes are touching.

It is one of the least used assembly commands but can become useful when it is vital to have curved faces touching.

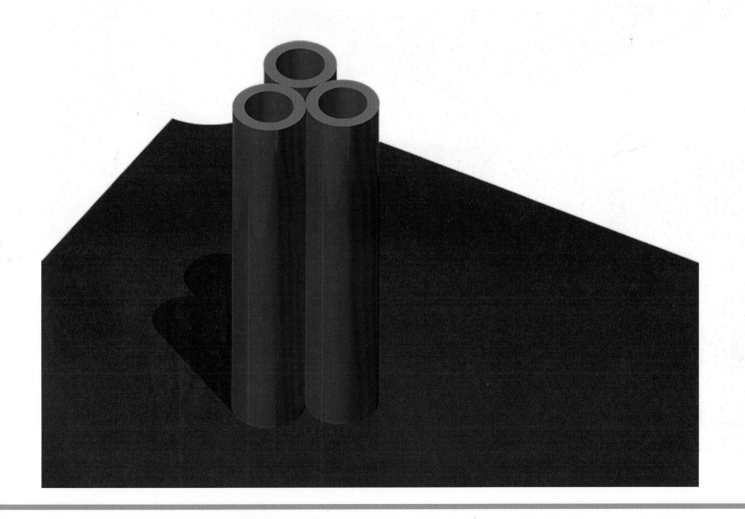

An assembly is a file or 3D CAD model in which two or more parts have been put together to create a complete model of an object.

The footstool shown here was assembled from component parts, which were 3D modelled individually.

There are many advantages of creating 3D CAD assembly files from the individual parts. The moving parts of a model can be simulated within the 3D CAD assembly model and can be animated to show how they work. The materials used for each of the parts can be tested for strength to ascertain whether they are strong enough for the job.

Exploded views are easy to produce from a 3D CAD assembly model. They show engineers how the items in the drawing can be fitted together for manufacture. They are often used in flat pack assembly instructions to help people build their furniture.

Sub-assembly

A sub-assembly is an assembly file that is placed into another assembly file.

In the example shown here, each of the items in the room have been modelled and assembled before being assembled together in the room.

Creating a suitable environment to show items in context is an important part of Higher Graphic Communication. You must develop your skills during your coursework so that you can create high-quality environments when it comes to the assignment.

 Assignment Advice

It is likely that you will need to produce an environment during your assignment. Ensure that all the parts of the room are in proportion to each other. For example, you will lose marks if you place a seat at a table and there is not enough room for a person's legs. Measure real life items of furniture to get an idea of appropriate sizes.

Stock or library components – CAD libraries

Libraries of premade 3D CAD models are available. These can be accessed through websites or as part of the software program you use.

These CAD libraries save time and effort as the user does not have to create all the components they require from scratch. They also ensure that where standard components are used, they will all be identical.

The scene below uses library components to help show the teapot in context on a stall at a trade fair. Using these components allows the user to make use of other people's expertise and ensures a high-quality production.

 Assignment Advice

Make sure you identify any models in your environment that were sourced from a CAD library, as you cannot be assessed on them.

3D CAD MODELLING

3D CAD views

Solid model

A solid model view provides a realistic view of a 3D CAD model. Any decals or colour that have been added will be visible on the model. Decals are images that can be added to a 3D CAD model. They will take the form of the model and can be positioned and sized to the user's needs. Materials, reflections and shadows are less obvious and of a poorer quality than on the fully-rendered final version of the product.

Wireframe

Wireframe views can be useful to see the structure of a 3D model. It can be more difficult to understand the shape of an object in a wireframe compared to a solid model, but it will show internal detail better. They can help the CAD user to build complex models and ensure parts fit together properly.

Rendered model

Professional rendering of a 3D model is completed using a specialist rendering package. This provides a photorealistic view of the 3D model that can be used in advertising. Often the product will be placed in a suitable environment to enhance the look of it. Shadows, reflections and textures are all shown to create a highly realistic graphic.

3D CAD rendering techniques

You will use a number of different rendering techniques when producing promotional graphics. You will set different light sources, add materials to the CAD models, show reflections and shadows and place the model in a suitable environment.

The example below shows an environment for the advertisement of a teapot. The list on the left-hand side shows the different light sources used. The user has specified that shadows will be cast by the light sources. They can also set how bright and what colour each light should be. Any reflective surfaces will show light bouncing from them in a realistic way.

The environment below is shown with wallpaper, carpet and a glass window and offers realistic representations of the materials within the scene.

The materials used in a scene will affect how strong the reflections are and the strength of each of the lights will determine how the shadows appear.

While 3D modelling packages will allow the user to render projects, the quality tends to be fairly poor.

Highly realistic and effective scenes can be created with specialist rendering software.

GO! Assignment Advice

For the best quality, use specialist rendering software to produce your environment.

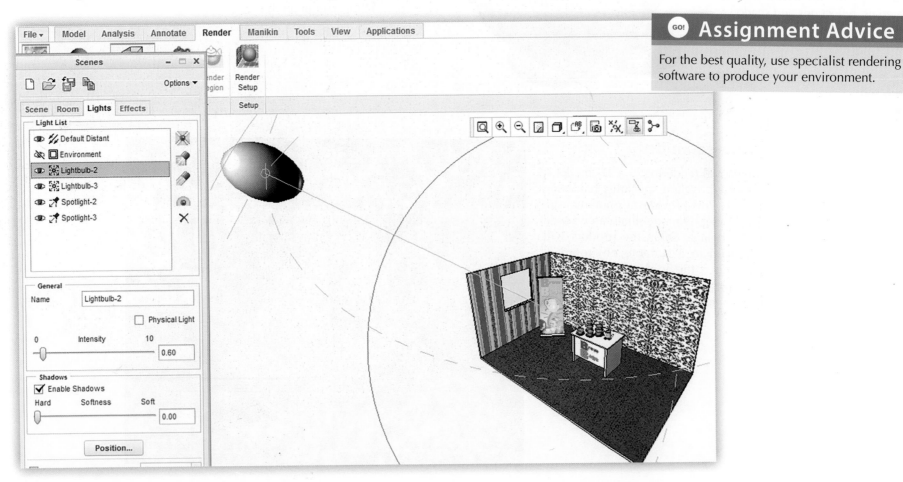

Terms involved in 3D modelling

To use 3D modelling software effectively, and to describe the process accurately, you must be able to use the correct terms.

Faces

Faces are the flat or curved surfaces of a 3D model.

Edges

An edge is the line where two faces meet at an angle.

Vertices

A vertex is a point (corner) on a 3D modelled object where two or more edges meet.

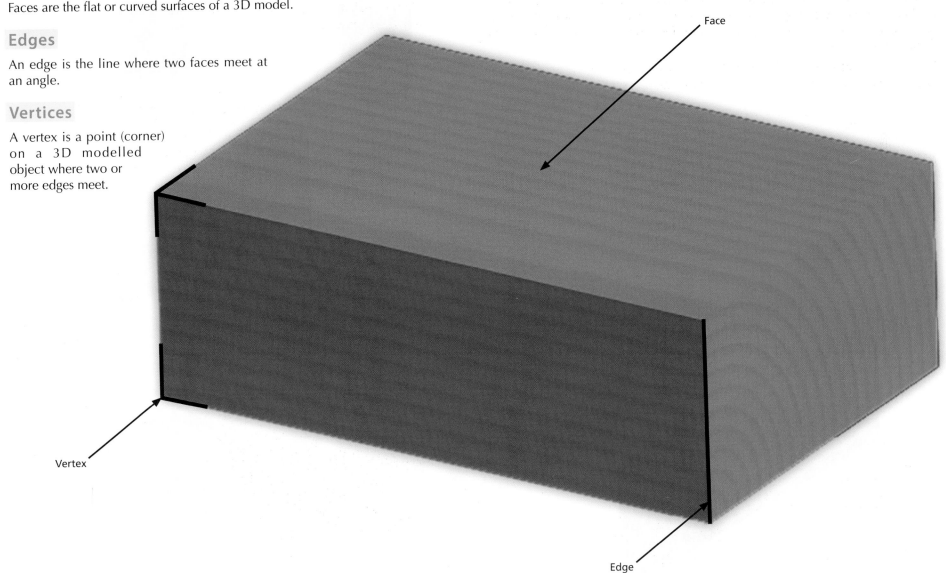

Face

Vertex

Edge

Modelling concepts

Bottom-up modelling

When an object is created by 3D modelling the component pieces separately and then assembling them, it is known as bottom-up modelling.

In this example the different parts of a child's peg toy have been produced separately as individual parts.

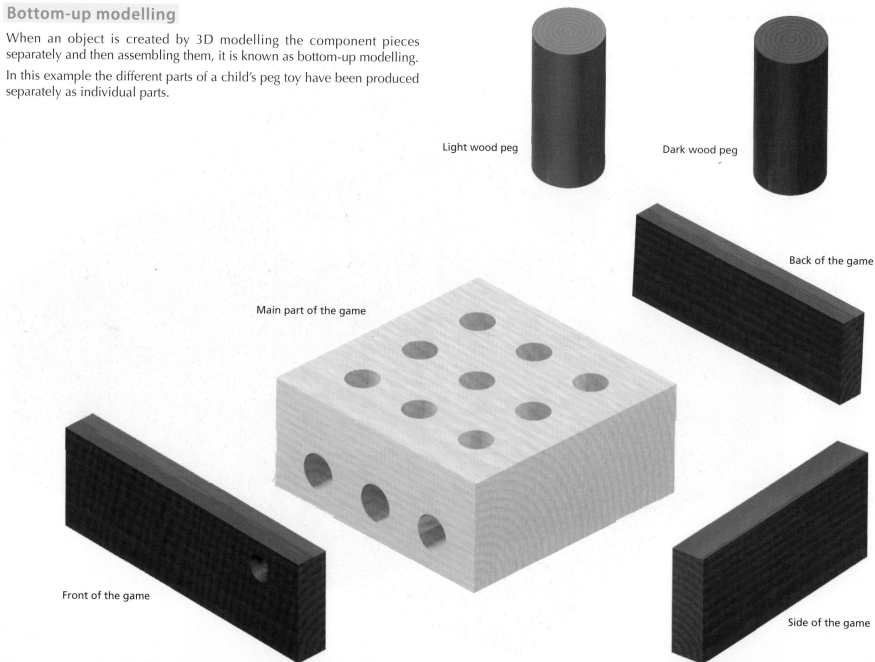

Light wood peg

Dark wood peg

Back of the game

Main part of the game

Front of the game

Side of the game

The different parts of the toy are then assembled using the centre align, mate and align tools.

This method is called 'bottom-up' because you build all of the parts required first and then move onto creating the assembly.

Top-down modelling

When the different parts of a 3D model are built within an assembly around an existing part, it is described as top-down modelling.

This is useful when working with library parts. Some parts of the model can be created in context in order to ensure they accurately fit in place. For example, when a designer is developing new flat pack furniture, the knock-down fittings that will be used to assemble the pieces together are supplied in standard sizes. This means that some parts of the furniture can be modeled around the fittings to ensure they fit.

While in an assembly, the user can create a new part. This will be saved as a part drawing, which can be edited individually at a later time if required.

When using top-down modelling, a part is created in context. The other views are ghosted (greyed out) so that the user can see the new part clearly and still use the edges of the other parts of the models. The project tool is extremely useful when creating the part in context, as you can use the lengths from the other parts to ensure accuracy.

A glass, which is to be filled with water, is shown here.

To render this realistically, the water needs to be modelled as a separate part. To ensure that the water fits exactly in the glass, the water has to be created in context using top-down modelling.

First, the glass has to be opened in an assembly file and the option to create a part in the assembly is selected by the user.

The elevation of the glass is shown here.

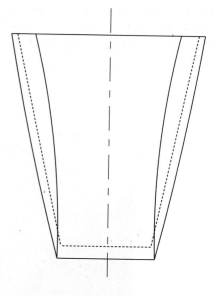

When sketching in context, the outline of the shape is greyed out while the new sketch is drawn. A solid can then be created from the sketch. In this case, the sketch will be revolved to create the water.

Shown is the profile and centre axis for the water to be placed in the glass. The profile will revolve through 360° to create the solid for the water.

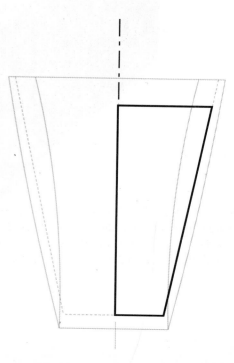

3D CAD MODELLING

When creating a model in context, the other models are greyed out while the new model is created. This makes it clearer to see the part you are working on while top-down modelling.

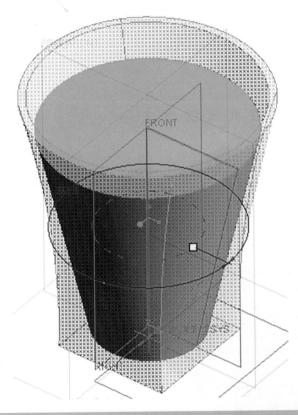

🔵 Exam Tip

Top-down modelling means that you can ensure new parts will fit exactly into an assembly. Parts of sketches that have been created based on existing dimensions using the project tool will automatically have their sizes updated if other parts are modified.

🔵 Assignment Advice

Modelling a glass filled with water can be an excellent addition to the environment you need to create in the assignment. Furthermore, you could use a loft and a revolve while creating the glass. This would allow you to cover two of the modelling techniques required to gain maximum marks in the 3D CAD modelling section of the assignment prior to creating the parts of the model to meet the assignment brief.

Once the part is created it will be displayed in context in the assembly. In this example, the water has been shown in the assembly with the glass.

Modelling tree/hierarchy

A modelling tree or hierarchy shows the different stages followed when a 3D CAD model is produced. This is shown at the side of the model.

It is a very useful tool as it allows you to edit specific parts of your model without having to start the entire thing again. This speeds up the process of developing graphics and provides the opportunity to make real-time changes to the product.

It also allows you to move some of the features so that they occur earlier or later in the model. This can be particularly useful when dealing with the shell command.

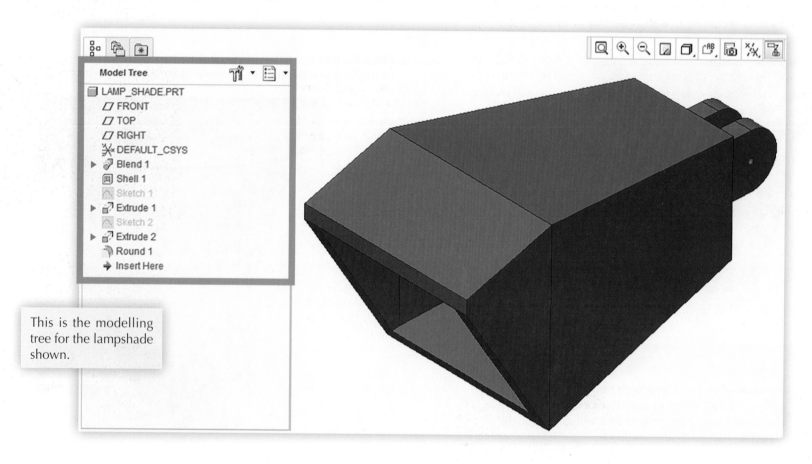

This is the modelling tree for the lampshade shown.

3D CAD MODELLING

136

Modelling plan

A modelling plan helps the user to create the 3D CAD model. It should show the sizes used for sketches and features and the order in which the model is created.

You need to create a modelling plan to meet one of the assessment standards for Higher Graphic Communication, as well as to show your understanding of how the software works.

You can produce a modelling plan prior to creating a 3D CAD model and use this as evidence. Alternatively, you can produce a modelling plan to describe the stages you went through when creating the 3D CAD model, using screen shots to help illustrate the process.

A modelling plan for how to create a lampshade is shown here.

Step 1

The main solid of the lampshade is created using lofting.

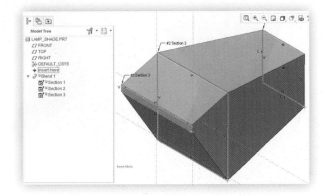

Step 2

The solid is shelled to a thickness of 15 mm. The front face is selected to open it up.

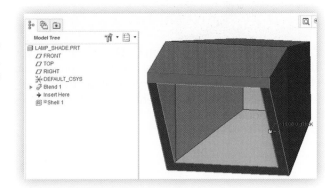

Step 3

The back of the lampshade is sketched then extruded to length.

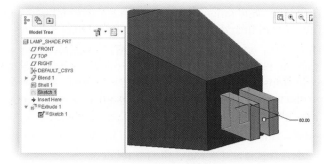

Step 4

A circle is sketched onto the side of this solid then extruded through both solids to subtract material.

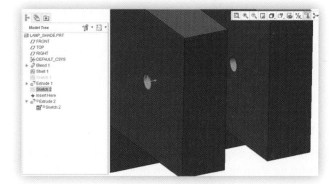

Step 5

The corners of the two solids have a fillet applied to 30mm.

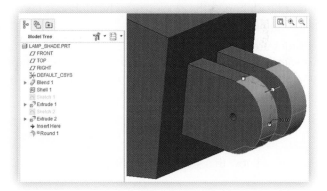

3D CAD MODELLING

137

CAD file types

There is a wide range of file types that are useful when producing graphics. They are all linked to various types of drawing packages and purposes.

There is a wide variety of 3D CAD programs that you can use while studying Higher Graphic Communication. Each of these have their own file extensions for the different drawings, models and renderings that can be produced. For the purpose of the exam you only need to know about the two below:

- **dxf** – This is the file extension used by AutoCAD® for drawings.
- **3ds** – This is a 3DS Max® file for renders.

GO! Exam Tip

Regardless of the software you may use at your centre, you only need to know that a dxf file is a drawing file and that a 3ds file is a file type for a rendered image.

step/iges

Step and iges files can be used by any 3D CAD package. This makes them useful for sharing files between different users. During your coursework, you may have used step files. For example, if you have produced a stand for a pair of headphones, the stock pair of headphones from the SQA is supplied as a step file.

Iges files are an older type of generic 3D CAD file format. They do not have the same information stored in them, such as the volume of an object, and have stopped being developed. Step files have largely replaced this type of file format.

GO! Exam Tip

You must know that step and iges files are universal 3D CAD file types.

stl

An stl file is a stereolithography file. It converts the mathematical file of the 3D CAD model into triangles. In turn, this allows the CAD model to be physically produced using rapid prototyping or CAD/CAM techniques.

Below is a rendered image of a perfume bottle with the stl file on the right.

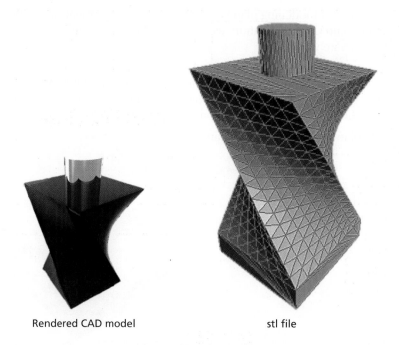

Rendered CAD model   stl file

GO! Exam Tip

Physical models produced from CAD models are a type of technical graphic. They can be used to show a real, physical representation of a product for the client to evaluate before full production begins. Larger 3D printers can be used to produce items ready to be sent to market with only small amounts of finishing required.

CAD libraries

A CAD library is a collection of commonly used shapes and symbols.

They help the user in a number of different ways. They save time and effort, as the user does not have to redraw each shape or symbol every time it is required. They also ensure that the British Standard symbols are used. Where stock parts are required in the design of a product, they ensure that those parts are used consistently.

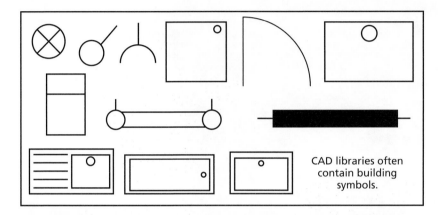

CAD libraries often contain building symbols.

Online CAD libraries will give a selection of components depending on your search criteria.

Online CAD libraries

There are online resources where users can search for stock components. These CAD libraries are stored online and allow members of the online community to upload any CAD model they have created so that it can be reused by other users.

When using these libraries, you can refine your searches by file type. As step/iges files can be used with any 3D CAD program, searching for these types of files when looking for existing models will ensure that you can use them in your work.

You can use models from online CAD libraries to help build environments for your CAD work throughout the course and in your assignment. If you do use these library models in your work, make sure that you reference where you got them from.

 **Assignment Advice**

Registering your details with online CAD libraries is free and will help you produce the environment for your assignment. Search for and download step files as these can be used with any 3D modelling package.

GO! Exam Tip

CAD libraries are a collection of commonly used symbols or 3D CAD models. They save the user time by allowing them to select components they require without having to produce them all individually.

BIG SMOKE
HELICOP

Chapter 7

Desktop Publishing

You will learn

- Desktop publishing
- Planning the layout of promotional graphics
- Planning strategies

- Visuals and annotation
- Proofs (pre-press)
- Magazine page features

Desktop publishing

Desktop publishing (DTP) is computer software widely used to produce promotional graphics.

The biggest difference between books and magazines is that magazines have to make the information contained within their pages attractive to look at to incite interest. Magazines are as much about entertaining their audience as they are about informing them.

Magazines are not the only type of publication that make use of DTP. Any type of advertising or communication with customers can be improved with the effective use of DTP. Business cards, bookmarks, roller banners or the interfaces used on touch screen devices are all examples of publications that utilise the design elements, design principles and features of desktop publishing.

Almost every home computer has a DTP package installed on it, which allows a huge number of people to be able to produce some kind of DTP document. There are also websites available that allow people to produce promotional graphics without any knowledge of how to structure an effective promotional document because they provide a variety of templates to use.

There are a large number of terms associated with DTP. The differences between some word processing packages and DTP packages are small. This means most people will be familiar with some of these terms. However, there can be no doubt that it is better to use a DTP package when producing visual layouts.

GO! Assignment Advice

Practise and experiment with how you can use the different DTP features and commands in your presentations to make them look professional.

Text box

A text box is an area into which you can add text. The text will follow the shape of the box if you choose to resize it.

The text box can take the form of any shape you like.

Text boxes can be any shape with text set to follow the confines of the shape.

Text boxes can be any shape with text set to follow the confines of the shape.

Text boxes can be any shape with text set to follow the confines of the shape.

Handles

Anytime you select an object in a DTP package, a frame will appear around it. These frames have handles at the corners and the midpoints to allow them to be resized.

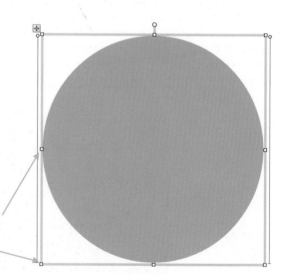

These are the handles for the frame.

Colour fill

Colour fill allows a shape to be filled with a colour specified by the user. There are a number of fill options for colour, e.g. a solid colour, gradient or texture.

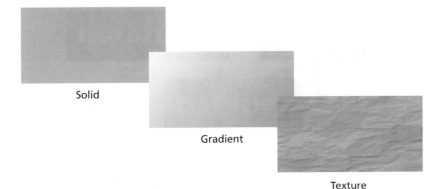

Solid

Gradient

Texture

Colour picking

The colour picking tool allows a colour from an image to be sampled and used in any other feature on the DTP presentation. On this business card for a local golf club, the colour of the flag has been picked and used for the colour of the text. This helps to ensure an accent colour is used throughout the presentation to improve its rhythm.

The colour picker icon is often shown as a dropper in DTP packages.

18

Golf

Fitness Friendship Competition

Contact your local club for details on how you can play.

Textured fill

There are a range of textures that can be applied to a shape when using DTP software. These can be used to improve a presentation in compliance with the design element, texture.

Gradient fill

A gradient fill shows one colour gradually fading to another. The user can adjust the settings to control the colours, pattern and direction of the gradient fill.

This is an effective method of adding tone to a presentation to give it form.

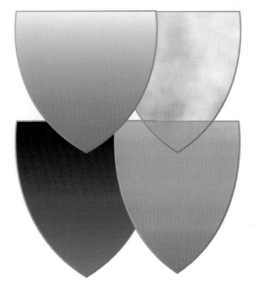

Text wrap

When text follows the edge of an image, it is described as being 'wrapped'. This is a useful method of incorporating images into your presentations and creating rhythm.

There are different types of text wrap available to use in DTP software and you should try to use the most appropriate one. You can see that the text here has been set to wrap around the right-hand side of the image.

Here the text has been set to wrap around the left-hand side of the image.

It is also possible to edit the position of the wrap points around an image. You can see the points are displayed around the image shown here. These can be moved to suit your requirements.

Reverse

Where there is a strong contrast between the colour of the background and the text, it is called 'reverse text'.

These are all examples of reverse text.

Reverse text

Reverse text

Reverse text

Extended text

This is the term given to long sections of body text.

The shaded areas here would be the extended text of a magazine article.

FEATURE

Light
it's in your hands

We take a look at the impact torches have had on our world.

Initially, torches were made from wood, with one end from flammable material to give light from fire. Over the ages this has evolved until now electricity powers our torches today.

Possible the most famous torch in the world, the Olympic Torch, was burned throughout the duration of the games, originally held in Ancient Greece. It commemorates the theft of fire from the Greek god Zeus by Prometheus and was introduced to the Olympics in 1928.

If a torch is made of sulphur mixed with lime, the fire will not diminish after being plunged into water. Such torches were used by the Ancient Romans and would quite possibly have been useful for discovering geological treasures hidden underground.

Torches have also been used in symbolism for generations. It is the symbol of enlightenment and can most famously be found being held by the Statue of Liberty.

Modern, electric torches come in many different forms but have improved the supply of light. Head torches used by miners are a safer alternative than paraffin lamps previously used.

Interestingly, torches have even given whole communities identities. The people of Newcastle and Sunderland have a famous rivalry, with their nicknames based on the manufactures

of the lamps used by miners. The coal miners in Newcastle were provided with 'Geordie' safety lamps designed by George Stephenson in 1815, while the coal miners in Wearside would make them (make'em) themselves. Hence, Newcastle folk are known as Geordies while residents of Sunderland are referred to as Mackems.

Large spotlights, like the one pictured, help searches for missing persons and tiny key ring torches which use high-power LEDs can help folk find their way home after a night's entertainment. Modern design has improved how we are able to see in darkness. Night has almost become day in our ever frantic world.

A brief history of light

Light has been a staple part of human life throughout time. So when did the major breakthroughs happen?

70000 BC - Animal fat burned to create light.
3050 BC - Egyptians invent the candle.
1780 - Oil lamp first produced.
1807 - Fluorescent lamp first demonstrated.
1880 - Edison produces 16W lightbulb, lasting 1500 hours.
1962 - LEDs developed.
1991 - Phillips invents efficient lightbulb lasting 60000 hours.

"The people of Newcastle and Sunderland have a famous rivalry, with their nicknames based on lamps"

Large spotlights, like this one by UCTorches, help missing people searches.

Dr I. Ball is an expert on torches and led to the design team responsible for the new spotlight from UCTorches.

Flow text along a path

Text can be set to follow a line or shape.

The flow text function can be used to make the text follow the shape of an image in a presentation, which can help achieve unity.

Copy and paste

Copy and paste can be used to repeat an image or frame somewhere else within the document.

Cut and paste

Cut and paste can be used to remove an image or frame from one document or part of the page to another.

Orientation

Orientation refers to the direction of the page, which is usually selected at the beginning of creating a new document. There are two possible orientations:

Landscape

Portrait

Line-spacing

The space between lines of text can be enlarged to make it easier to read. This only works to a point, after which the text becomes disconnected and more difficult to read. Conversely, line spacing can also be made smaller to help fit more information into an area of a presentation.

> This text has double line spacing.
>
> You can see that the distance
>
> between the lines is larger, which
>
> can make it easier to read or put
>
> handwritten notes into.

> This text has condensed line spacing. You can see that this makes it more difficult to read, but that more text can be fitted into a smaller space. This is often used for the small print on contracts.

Transparency

The transparency setting allows objects in a DTP document to be made see-through.

The amount of transparency can be changed to suit the needs of the user.

In the example here, a transparency has been added behind the company logo to make it easier to read on the backdrop of the image.

Cropping (square and full cropping)

The crop tool can be used to remove the outer portions of an image, making it smaller in size. Square cropping is the most simple form. It is often applied to screen grabs, so that only the relevant part is shown.

Full cropping is where only the required part of an image is left. The rest of the image is removed. Usually this requires work in photo editing software to be successful.

The two images below compare the two types of cropping. The image of the MP3 player on the left has been square cropped. The one on the right has been fully cropped to the outline of the MP3 player.

This is the original poster.

Square cropping

Full cropping

DESKTOP PUBLISHING

Drop shadow

When a shadow is applied behind text or an image it is called a drop shadow. This will add depth by making it look like the object is coming off the page.

DTP software allows the user to edit the various aspects of the shadow such as its intensity, direction, colour and sharpness.

It is a simple yet effective way of adding depth to a page.

DROP SHADOW

GO! Assignment Advice

Study the layouts of a wide range of magazines in order to help you develop your own ideas. You can either buy these or use free magazine or newsstand apps.

Rotate

The rotate setting allows you to turn an image through an angle. The user can select from preset angles or has the option to input any angle they require.

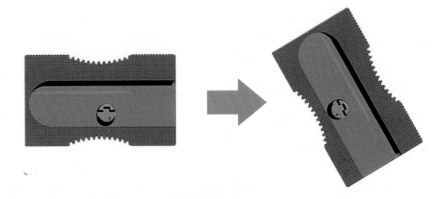

Paper sizing

The physical size of a page can be altered. A smaller page size can be used to reduce printing and transport costs. This can also make a magazine or newspaper easier to read and carry. Some layouts need to be larger in size, like roller banners or large posters.

The most common set of paper sizes in use are the ISO A sizes. These range from A0 (the largest) to A8. The size is reduced by half each time.

In school, A4 and A3 paper are the most frequently used paper sizes.

A4 paper is 297 × 210 mm.

A3 paper is 420 × 297 mm.

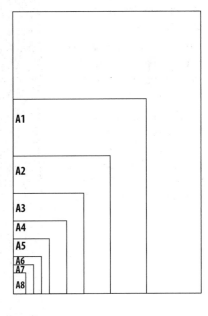

Alignment

There are four main types of alignment:

1. Left alignment

2. Right alignment

3. Justified

4. Centred

Alignment should be used to help create and maintain rhythm in a presentation. Where sections of text belong together, or where text belongs with an image, alignment can be used to help show this relationship.

Look at how alignment is used in the magazine layout opposite:

The blue areas of the pull quote and floating element are right aligned with each other.

The headline and the body text are left aligned.

The image of the torch is centred on the page and centred with the text in the middle column.

All of this gives the layout structure and makes it easy to read and understand.

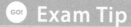

GO! Exam Tip

If you are asked about alignment in your exam, make sure you refer to a specific type of alignment in your answer. Simply saying object A is aligned with object B is not enough to gain you marks.

FEATURE

Light
it's in your hands

We take a look at the impact torches have had on our world.

Initially, torches were made from wood, with one end from flammable material to give light from fire. Over the ages this has evolved until now electricity powers our torches today.

Possible the most famous torch in the world, the Olympic Torch, was burned throughout the duration of the games, originally held in Ancient Greece. It commemorates the theft of fire from the Greek god Zeus by Prometheus and was introduced to the Olympics in 1928.

If a torch is made of sulphur mixed with lime, the fire will not diminish after being plunged into water. Such torches were used by the Ancient Romans and would quite possibly have been useful for discovering geological treasures hidden underground. Torches have also been used in symbolism for generations. It is the symbol of enlightenment and can most famously be found being held by the Statue of Liberty.

Modern, electric torches come in many different forms but have improved the supply of light. Head torches used by miners are a safer alternative than paraffin lamps previously used.

Interestingly, torches have even given whole communities identities. The people of Newcastle and Sunderland have a famous rivalry, with their nicknames based on the manufactures

of the lamps used by miners. The coal miners in Newcastle were provided with 'Geordie' safety lamps designed by George Stephenson in 1815, while the coal miners in Wearside would make them (make'em) themselves. Hence, Newcastle folk are known as Geordies while residents of Sunderland are referred to as Mackems.

Large spotlights, like the one pictured, help searches for missing persons and tiny key ring torches which use high-power LEDs can help folk find their way home after a night's entertainment. Modern design has improved how we are able to see in darkness. Night has almost become day in our ever frantic world.

A brief history of light

Light has been a staple part of human life throughout time. So when did the major breakthroughs happen?

70000 BC - Animal fat burned to create light.
3000 BC - Egyptians invent the candle
1780 - Oil lamp first produced
1867 - Fluorescent lamp first demonstrated.
1880 - Edison produces 16W lightbuld, lasting 1500 hours.
1962 - LEDs developed.
1991 - Phillips envents efficient lightbulb lasting 60000 hours.

"The people of Newcastle and Sunderland have a famous rivalry, with their nicknames based on lamps"

Large spotlights, like this one by UCTorches, help missing people searches.

Dr I. Ball is an expert on torches and led to the design team responsible for the new spotlight from UCTorches.

16   LIGHT AND LUMINATION   ISSUE 207

Single- and multi-page formats

Multi-page layouts include magazines, folding leaflets and table top advertising. They all consist of more than one page.

Folding leaflets must be set up carefully to ensure the margins and grid structures match on both sides.

Examples of single-page layouts are posters and business cards. These layouts are often best kept simple to have strong visual impact.

Justification

Even though they are similar, there is a difference between alignment and justification that you should be aware of. Alignment is how different parts of a layout line up with one another. Justification refers only to text and how it is set out.

Text can be justified in four ways:

1. Left justification

2. Right justification

3. Centre justification

4. Full justification

Left-justified text begins
each line at the left margin.

Right-justified text begins each
line at the right margin.

Centre-justified text is measured
from the centre of
the column or page.

Fully-justified text is aligned to both the left- and right-hand margins as shown here. This can make the text look ordered and tidy. However, the gaps between the words and characters will be different on each line. This can make fully-justified text more difficult to read than text that is justified to only one side.

Grid

A grid is a pattern that the user can set on the DTP layout page, which helps to structure the layout.

Grids can be regular or irregular in pattern. The choice will be determined by the type of publication being produced. Formal layouts usually follow a strong grid structure, whereas informal layouts can use irregular layouts to have greater visual impact.

Snap

When you set up a grid or ruler guides, you can make the cursor snap to these marks as you create your DTP presentation. This speeds up the process of laying out your DTP work and can help to ensure alignment with images and text.

This shows a master page layer with a grid and guides. The cursor will snap to each of the red lines to help achieve accuracy and consistency of layout throughout a book.

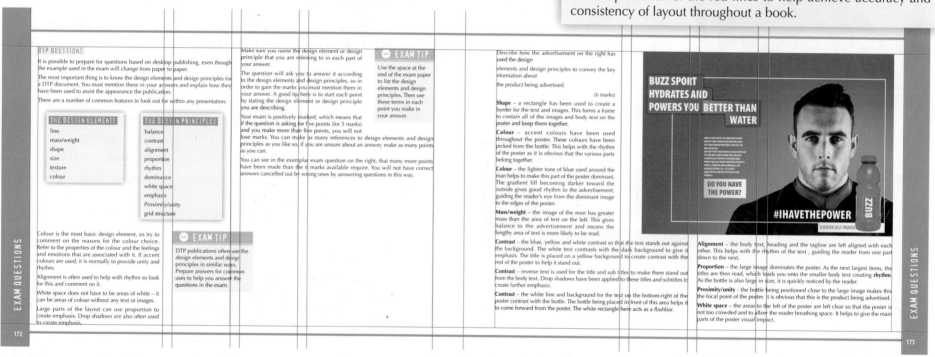

Guides

A guide is a line that is shown on the screen to help position text or graphics. These lines are not printed in the final version of the document.

Master page layers

Layers are parts of a DTP document, which contain the different elements of the presentation. You can view the individual layers, a selection of layers or all the layers together.

Master pages allow you to structure all of the pages in a magazine or book on the same grid format. These allow consistency of layout to be achieved easily.

Serif and sans serif

There are two families of font available for you to use: serif fonts and sans serif fonts.

Serif fonts tend to be more traditional and formal, while sans serif fonts are more modern and informal.

Serif fonts have small serif (small lines) on the ends of each letter. Sans serif fonts do not have these serifs. The term 'sans serifs' means 'without serifs'.

These are serifs

Sans Serif

Font styles

Font styles can be used to infer the use and target market of the product being advertised or a feeling or emotion.

Childlike

Horror

Love

ELECTRONIC

Medieval

Futuristic

Indent

An indent is where a selected part of body text starts further in from the left margin than the rest of the text.

> This piece of text has been indented by 20 mm from the left margin.

Indents can be used to highlight parts of text that may be of particular interest to the reader or to show the start of a new paragraph.

Hanging indent

A hanging indent is where the first line of text is not indented, but the rest of the lines are. These are commonly found where there are lists. A useful application of this is in a DTP presentation when describing the product specification of an item.

> Often pupils back up their school work using a USB memory stick. This is because:
> - it is portable
> - it has large storage capabilities
> - it is cheap.

Drop caps

Using the drop caps feature highlights the first capital letter of a passage and makes it bigger. This makes the first letter stand out, giving it impact and helping to lead the article on from the larger subheading text.

In this weeks edition of Beatz, we look at the rise of Scottish DJ 'DeeJay Choon' and how one track has elevated him from unknown to an international superstar.

Running headline

A running headline is a header that appears on each page of a DTP document. It can also be referred to as a running header. Running headlines often contain the title of the book or chapter or the name of the magazine.

Study guide	DTP terms

Import/export

When creating DTP documents it is possible to import or export different types of files.

You can import pdf files into some DTP software packages for editing and can also import images.

It is also possible to export files from a DTP document. For example, you can publish an entire DTP document as a pdf file so that it can be viewed using any computer. This function can also be used to export a DTP document as an image file.

DTP Layers

The different parts of a layout are called layers and can be ordered to create the best possible effect. Parts of a layer can be partially hidden behind other layers or brought to the front.

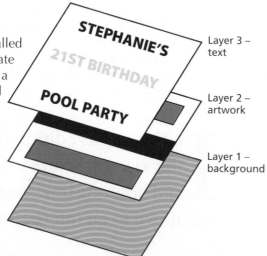

Layer 3 – text

Layer 2 – artwork

Layer 1 – background

Planning the layout of promotional graphics

Before you can produce your final presentation you should plan different ideas for how it will look.

This will enable you to explore various possibilities so that you can create the most effective possible layout.

Creating new ideas is difficult, so you might find the process described over the next few pages useful.

GO! Assignment Advice

Use existing layouts to help you create your own.

Higher order thinking skills

- Creating
- Evaluating
- Analysing
- Applying
- Understanding
- Remembering

Lower order thinking skills

DESKTOP PUBLISHING

Planning strategies

When a client approaches a graphic designer to complete some work for them, they will give the designer a brief. This brief will outline the type of graphics required, their purpose and the target audience. Only if the brief is well written by the client will the graphic designer be able to produce a range of suitable images.

A structured method of planning layouts can help you to produce high-quality presentations:

1. Thumbnails

2. Visuals

3. Proofs

Thumbnails

Thumbnails are quickly produced ideas for the layout of a presentation. The examples shown here have been produced using manual methods, but thumbnails can be produced using electronic methods. From the initial ideas produced at this stage, some will be developed into the visuals produced using DTP software.

Using a curved line to separate the company name from the rest of the presentation helps give it dominance.

Using the image of the teapot at an angle helps to break the formality of the structure to give it impact and emphasis.

Bleed used for the teapot will attract attention to the product.

Using the lines through the diagonals will add to the rhythm of the layout and give the company name dominance over the layout.

Including the company logo is important to promote the brand.

Using a flashbar behind the teapot will bring it forward to give it prominence.

This is a simple layout structure, which is clear and effective.

The position of the company logo between the text will add unity between these areas.

The contrasting colours used with the teapot and background make the image more eye catching.

The areas of text are right aligned with each other to give the presentation good rhythm.

The company name is positioned centrally to allow it to dominate the layout and connect all the elements.

Visuals and annotation

Visuals are better quality representations of the final idea for the presentation. They are produced using DTP software to give a quality output at speed. The images used at this stage may be of a lower quality than in the final presentation.

 Assignment Advice

Save the different stages of DTP layouts as different files in order to easily include them in your assignment to show the evolution of your layout accompanied by your evaluation annotations.

Annotating the visuals as they are produced can help you to improve the structure and organisation of the thoughts and processes that naturally take place. This makes it easier for you to make the appropriate improvements and optimise the evolutionary process.

Version 1

Company colour scheme has been applied throughout the presentation.

Brew Bags images used to promote the product identity.

Text and company name is left aligned to create rhythm.

Asymmetrical alignment is used to create movement and interest.

Teapot placed in front of arcs to create depth.

Teapot contrasting with the company colours to create impact.

Version 2

Brew Bags name prominent at the top of the poster. There may not be enough contrast between the name and the background for it to stand out.

Drop shadow added to teapot to create depth.

Large, dominant image of the product to create impact and be eye catching.

Large positive image of the target market to create dominance and positive feeling toward the product.

Left-aligned text to help rhythm.

Brew Bags logo bleeds onto page to create impact.

Version 3

Centre alignment has been used with the Brew Bags name, the teapot, the slogan and the image at the bottom of the presentation to create rhythm. This leads the viewer from the top to the bottom of the banner quickly.

A drop shadow has been added to the teapot and the text to make them stand out. The use of dark and light drop shadows helps to differentiate the teapot from the slogan. The light drop shadow makes the slogan easier to read and makes it lighter in weight to give it the feeling that it is floating off the page.

The text has been turned at an angle to give a feeling of excitement to the presentation. This is eye catching and also leads the reader from word to word providing the presentation with rhythm.

The large brand name dominates the presentation which draws attention to it.

Positive image of target market bleeds into the bottom of the presentation to create impact and good balance.

A transparency has been added to the background to help the Brew Bags name contrast with it so that it can stand out.

The slogan above the teapot helps to present the teapot in a frame and separate it from the dominant company name at the top of the presentation.

Image of teapot overlaps the layer of the circles. This makes it stand out and creates unity between the top and bottom sections of the presentation.

Transparent white box displayed behind the logo to help it stand out against the image.

Product identity reinforced with the brand logo placed in the corner.

Proofs (pre-press)

Proofs are the final version of the presentation, which have to be checked by the customer and editors before going to print. Any mistakes must be picked up at this stage. The people who do this job must be very thorough in their checks and have a good eye for detail.

The proof is evaluated against the original brief and specification. Only if it meets the specification will it be deemed appropriate for a print run.

Brief

You need to develop preliminary, production and promotional graphics for a proposal for a teapot.

The graphics of the teapot must provide:

- Preliminary sketches that convey material, light and shade for the teapot designs
- Dimensioned orthographic drawings for the teapot
- Technical detail required to manufacture the teapot
- Pictorial line drawings of the teapot to help show non-technical people how it appears to fit together
- Promotional material to advertise the teapot. This should be a 150 × 600 mm roller banner that can be easily transported to be used at trade fairs and shopping centres
- Display the teapot in a suitable environment to show it in context

This layout meets the brief:

The image of the young women makes it obvious that the company is aiming the product at young people.

The Brew Bags logo and colours are used throughout the layout to emphasise the company identity or brand.

The use of text at angles creates impact and reflects the fresh look that this range of teapots is bringing to a traditional product.

The Brew Bags company font, Jagger SF, is used throughout the presentation.

The presentation shown is a scaled representation of the real-life roller banner.

Magazine page features

Magazines have their own particular set of features that can be used to make them attractive and have visual impact.

Headline

A headline is the main heading of the presentation. It is normally the largest text size on the sheet and dominates the other pieces of text.

Margin

The margins are the spaces between the columns and the left- and right-hand edges of the page.

Subheading

A subheading is usually included in a magazine layout. It is the part of the page that leads the reader from the title to the body text. It gives a short introduction to the content of the article.

Column

Columns are produced when text is set using ordered grid structures. There are many different ways of laying out the columns in a presentation. You should use the one that most suits the style you are trying to achieve.

Pull quote

A pull quote is a small section of text that is sampled and enlarged. This is then set into the layout as a way of attracting interest in the article. It is often set in italics or reverse to make it stand out. Often it is a controversial quote or an interesting part of the article to entice the reader.

Bleed

After printing, pages are trimmed to size. A bleed is when an image or element runs outside the margins of the page (beyond the crop marks). This means that when the page is trimmed, the artwork or element goes right to the edge of the page.

Gutter

A gutter is the gap between columns of text. It can be kept at a uniform distance for formal presentations or can be altered for more impact.

Column rule

A column rule is a line that runs between two columns to help separate the text. It is commonly used in formal magazine layouts where the text is small in size and tightly compacted.

Caption

A caption is a description or quote that accompanies an image.

Header and footer

A header is the space at the top of a presentation and a footer is the space at the bottom. On a multi-page layout like a book, it is common for the header and footer to be in the same style on every page.

Folio

The folio is the name given to the page number. This can be added to the presentation wherever you want, but is commonly part of the header or footer.

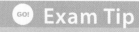

GO! Exam Tip

Ensure you can identify and describe these features as you can be asked about these in your exam.

Header

Headline

Light

it's in your hands

Right margin

Subheading

We take a look at the impact torches have had on our world.

Reverse

Column

Initially, torches were made from wood, with one end from flammable material to give light from fire. Over the ages this has evolved until now electricity powers our torches today.

Possible the most famous torch in the world, the Olympic Torch, was burned throughout the duration of the games, originally held in Ancient Greece. It commemorates the theft of fire from the Greek god Zeus by Prometheus and was introduced to the Olympics in 1928.

If a torch is made of sulphur mixed with lime, the fire will not diminish after being plunged into water. Such torches were used by the Ancient Romans and would quite possibly have been useful for discovering geological treasures hidden underground.

Torches have also been used in symbolism for generations. It is the symbol of enlightenment and can most famously be found being held by the Statue of Liberty.

Left margin

Modern, electric torches come in many different forms but have improved the supply of light. Head torches used by miners are a safer alternative than paraffin lamps previously used.

Interestingly, torches have even given whole communities identities. The people of Newcastle and Sunderland have a famous rivalry, with their nicknames based on the manufactures

Image

of the lamps used by miners. The coal miners in Newcastle were provided with 'Geordie' safety lamps designed by George Stephenson in 1815, while the coal miners in Wearside would make them (make'em) themselves. Hence, Newcastle folk are known as Geordies while residents of Sunderland are referred to as Mackems.

Large spotlights, like the one pictured, help searches for missing persons and tiny key ring torches which use high-power LEDs can help folk find their way home after a night's entertainment. Modern design has improved how we are able to see in darkness. Night has almost become day in our ever frantic world.

A brief history of light

Light has been a staple part of human life throughout time. So when did the major breakthroughs happen?

70000 BC - Animal fat burned to create light.
3000 BC - Egyptians invent the candle
1780 - Oil lamp first produced.
1867 - Fluorescent lamp first demonstrated.
1880 - Edison produces 16W lightbuld, lasting 1500 hours.
1962 - LEDs developed.
1991 - Phillips envents efficient lightbulb lasting 60000 hours.

Gutter

Floating element

"The people of Newcastle and Sunderland have a famous rivalry, with their nicknames based on lamps"

Pull quote

Dr I. Ball is an expert on torches and led to the design team responsible for the new spotlight from UCTorches.

Caption

Bleed

Large spotlights, like this one by UCTorches, help missing people searches.

Folio

Footer

DESKTOP PUBLISHING

157

Chapter 8

The Assessment Standards

You will learn

- **Meeting the assessment standards**
- **The combined approach – Brew Bags example**

Meeting the assessment standards

Your teacher will organise your course in a way that gives you the best possible chance of achieving a good grade.

They will set coursework that allows you to practise and prepare by structuring work in a similar way to how the assignment must be produced and develop your skills producing the types of drawing that will gain you marks.

Your teacher will also ensure you are ready for your exam by helping you understand the topics described within the Course Assessment Specification.

It can be helpful to use a handheld scanner to produce digital versions of hand-produced sketches, so they can be included in a computer-based folio. This will help keep the layout consistent throughout the graphic proposal.

The combined approach – Brew Bags example

You can meet the requirements of the course units in different ways. Using the combined approach will effectively prepare you for the assignment and allow you to gain the units through naturally-progressive project work.

Brew Bags is a project that meets the requirements for both the 2D Graphic Communication and 3D Graphic Communication units of the Higher Graphic Communication course. It is also designed to prepare candidates for the assignment.

The candidate must complete a range of drawings to make up a graphic proposal to successfully meet the brief.

These drawings should be both hand sketched and computer produced.

The evidence generated throughout this project should be kept together in a graphic proposal and saved onto the computer. This will allow each page to maintain a consistent company layout throughout.

Higher Graphic Communication

Brew Bags Teapots

Problem Situation

Brew Bags is a modern company looking to reinvigorate the tea brewing market.

60.2 billion cups of tea are drunk in Britain every year. Brew Bags would like to tap into this market in order to sell modern or traditional looking teapots to young people.

Brew Bags have identified that one of the needs of their market is that customers want to be able to customise their teapot. Therefore, their teapots must have interchangeable bases that can be attached using machine screws.

Your job is to provide the graphics that will be presented to the Brew Bags board in order to produce this product.

Brief

You need to develop preliminary, production and promotional graphics for a proposal for the teapot.

The graphics of the teapot must meet the following requirements:

- Preliminary sketches that convey material, light and shade for the teapot designs.
- Provide dimensioned orthographic drawings of the teapot.
- The technical detail required to manufacture the teapot.
- Pictorial line drawings of the teapot to help show non technical people how it appears and fits together.
- Promotional material to advertise the teapot. This should be a 1500 × 600 mm roller banner that can be easily transported to be used at trade fairs and shopping centres.
- Display the teapot in a suitable environment to show it in context.

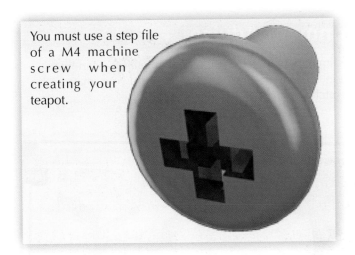

You must use a step file of a M4 machine screw when creating your teapot.

You can see that the brief specifies a range of details that must be used when completing the graphic proposal.

Brew Bags would like to develop their brand through their graphics. Therefore, it is very important to follow their instructions.

RGB colour values DARK BLUE:

R: 44   G: 49   B: 146

RGB colour values LIGHT BLUE:

R: 0   G: 255   B: 255

The Brew Bags company logo is shown here. It should appear throughout the folio and certainly on the promotional items. You can access this file from the network.

The font used by the company in their title and correspondence is Jagger SF. You should use this in your promotional graphic.

The RGB codes for the company colours are shown. These should also feature throughout the promotional material.

3D modelling commands

Part of the instructions is a list of 3D modelling commands that must be used when creating the solution for the teapot.

These are some of the required commands for Higher Graphic Communication.

They are described earlier in this book.

Information to consider before beginning the project.	Your teapot must have at least 3 parts.
	There is no limit to the 3D modelling features you can use when creating the teapot but you must use the following features:
	Extrude along a path (sweep along a path); **Loft** (blend); **Helix**.
	You should also use some of the following 3D modelling edits:
	Shell; Fillet; Chamfer; Mirror; Array; Add; Subtract; Intersect.

GO! Exam Tip

The words in bold are the terms you need to use in your exam.

Preliminary sketches are graphics that can be produced using both manual and electronic methods. They are used to show a range of possible solutions to a brief.

They give an idea of shape, material, form and texture to inform the client at the early stages of developing a product.

You should use a range of 3D graphic techniques when producing preliminary drawings.

There is no requirement for you to use all of the techniques listed below in one preliminary sheet.

GO! Assignment Advice

If producing preliminary graphics using manual methods, scan them and insert them into your computer-based folio. Crop your images then enhance your sketches using drop shadows or flashbars.

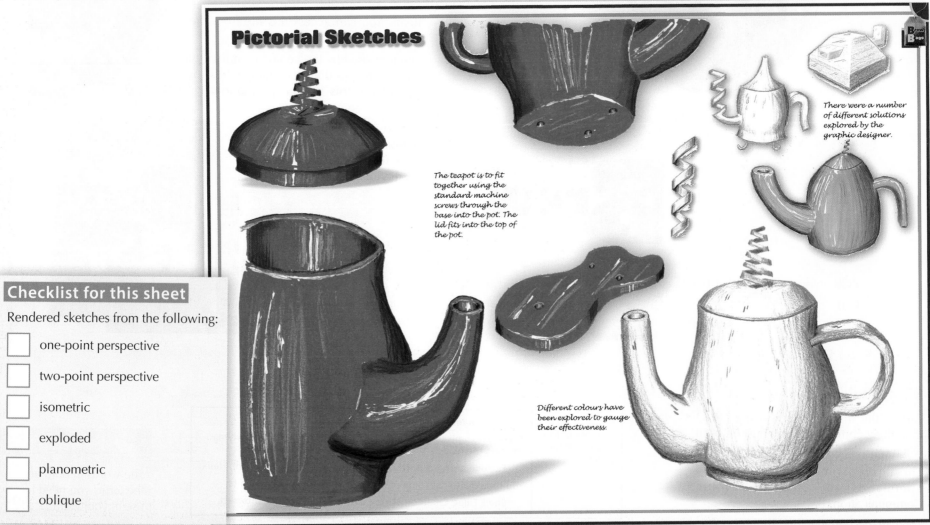

Pictorial Sketches

The teapot is to fit together using the standard machine screws through the base into the pot. The lid fits into the top of the pot.

There were a number of different solutions explored by the graphic designer.

Different colours have been explored to gauge their effectiveness.

Checklist for this sheet

Rendered sketches from the following:

- [ ] one-point perspective
- [ ] two-point perspective
- [ ] isometric
- [ ] exploded
- [ ] planometric
- [ ] oblique

Brew Bags – orthographic sketches

Your orthographic sketches must show sufficient dimensions to enable you to create the 3D models of the various components of your product, in this case the teapot.

Including the necessary dimensions needed to produce the product using 3D CAD software will make the modelling stage far easier.

These orthographic sketches must follow British Standard conventions and be sketched using third-angle projection.

By scanning the sketches and placing them into a DTP software program, it is possible to maintain a consistent approach to the graphic proposal. This is what the candidate has done here.

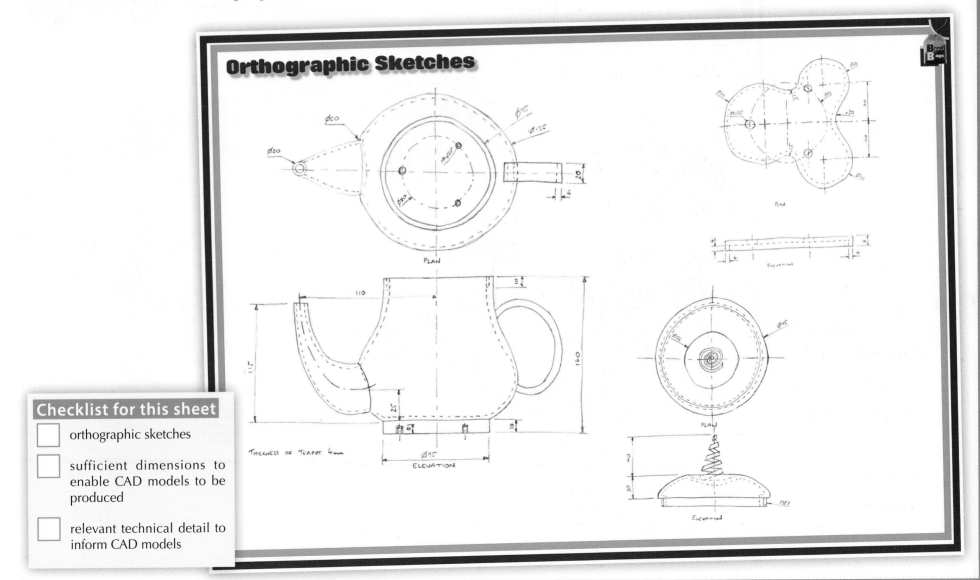

Checklist for this sheet

- [ ] orthographic sketches
- [ ] sufficient dimensions to enable CAD models to be produced
- [ ] relevant technical detail to inform CAD models

When planning the DTP layout, the candidate should show the development from the initial idea to the final layout, including the evaluation they have undertaken at each stage.

Using DTP software when planning the layouts will assist with the quality and speed of the planning process. You can annotate these plans in the DTP software too.

Make sure you give reasons for each choice you make. You must also give reasons for any changes.

It is vital that you use the correct terms for the design elements, design principles and DTP features throughout these annotations.

THE ASSESSMENT STANDARDS

Checklist for this sheet

- ☐ reference images used
- ☐ show different versions
- ☐ use the design elements and design principles in the annotations
- ☐ give reasons for changes
- ☐ use a scaled version of the layout

Preliminary Layouts

Image of ladies drinking tea originated from:

shutterstock.com

Image was edited to remove the background and saved as a .png to retain the transparency from the photo editing software.

Brew bags has a colour scheme as part of their branding. The RGB mixes of colours that should be used are.

Dark Blue: R44; G49; B146

Light Blue R0; G255; B255

The Brew bags logo and brand name should be used in the layout. These are available for use and are supplied as .png files.

Brew bags have also specified that the font **Jagger SF** should be used in their promotional material.

Company colour scheme has been applied throughout the presentation.

Brew bags images used to promote the product identity.

Customisable teapots

Text and company name is left aligned to create rhythm.

Asymmetrical alignment is used to create movement and interest.

What does your brew say about you?

Teapot placed in front of arcs to create depth.

Teapot contrasting with the company colours to create impact.

Brew Bags name prominent at the top of the poster. There may not be enough contrast between it and the background for it to stand out.

Drop shadow added to teapot in order to create depth.

Large, dominant image of the product to create impact and be eye catching.

Large positive image of the target market to create dominance and positive feeling toward the product.

Customise
Feeling
Love
Style
Life

Left aligned text to help rhythm.

Brew Bags logo bleeds onto page to create impact.

Centre alignment has been used with the Brew Bags name, the teapot, the slogan and the image at the bottom of the presentation to create rhythm. This leads the viewer from the top to the bottom of the banner quickly.

A drop shadow has been added tot he teapot and the text to make them stand out. The use of dark and light drop shadows helps to differentiate the teapot from the slogan. The light drop shadow makes the slogan easier to read and makes it lighter in weight to give it the feeling that it is floating off the page.

The text has been turned at an angle to give a feeling of excitement to the presentation. This is eye catching and also leads the reader from word to word providing the presentation with rhythm.

The large brand name dominates the presentation which draws attention to it.

A transparency has been added to the background to help the Brew Bags name contrast with it so that it can stand out.

The slogan above the teapot helps to present the teapot in a frame and separate it from the dominant company name at the top of the presentation.

Image of teapot overlaps the layer of the circles. This makes it stand out and creates unity between the top and bottom sections of the presentation.

Custom
Love
Feeling
Style
Life

Transparent white box displayed behind the logo to help it stand out against the image.

Positive image of target market bleeds into the bottom of the presentation to create impact and good balance.

Product identity reinforced with the brand logo placed in the corner.

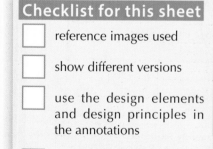

Brew Bags – component orthographics

In this case, the candidate has produced orthographic views of each part of the teapot.

As these are component views, they are dimensioned to allow manufacture. Other details such as centre lines, labels, a title block and a border must also be added to the drawing.

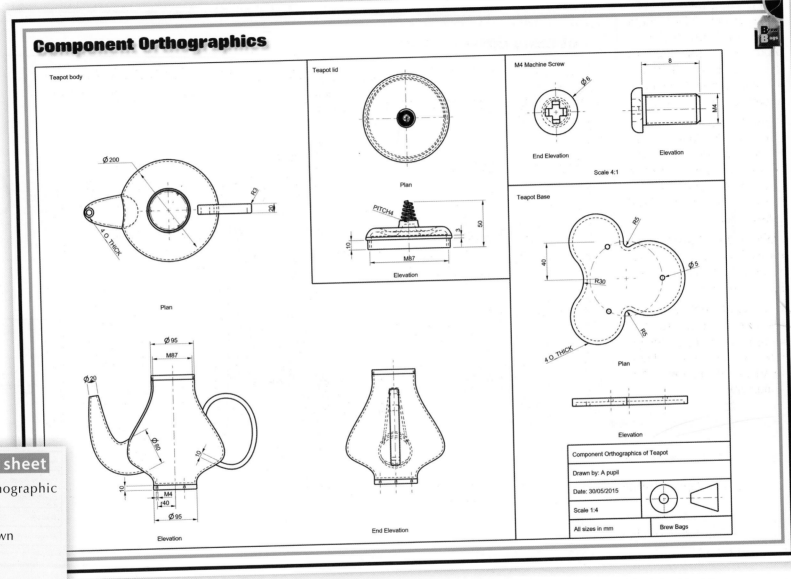

Component Orthographics

Teapot body

Ø 200
R3
4 O THICK

Plan

Ø 95
M87
Ø 20
Ø 80
10
10
M4
40
Ø 95

Elevation

End Elevation

Teapot lid

Plan

PITCH4
50
3
10
M87

Elevation

M4 Machine Screw

Ø6
8
M4

End Elevation   Elevation

Scale 4:1

Teapot Base

R5
40
Ø5
R30
R5
4 O THICK

Plan

Elevation

Component Orthographics of Teapot	
Drawn by: A pupil	
Date: 30/05/2015	
Scale 1:4	
All sizes in mm	Brew Bags

Checklist for this sheet

- [ ] component orthographic views shown
- [ ] hidden detail shown
- [ ] centre lines given
- [ ] dimensions shown
- [ ] border and title block

You must show a stepped sectional view and a detail view of the product.

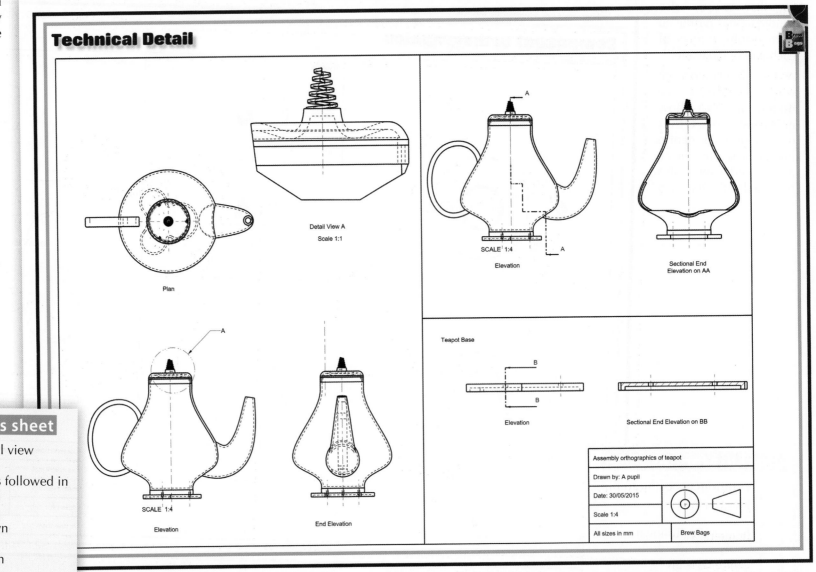

Technical Detail

Plan

Detail View A
Scale 1:1

SCALE 1:4

Elevation

Sectional End Elevation on AA

SCALE 1:4

Elevation

End Elevation

Teapot Base

Elevation

Sectional End Elevation on BB

Assembly orthographics of teapot	
Drawn by: A pupil	
Date: 30/05/2015	
Scale 1:4	
All sizes in mm	Brew Bags

Checklist for this sheet

- [ ] stepped sectional view
- [ ] British Standards followed in sections
- [ ] detail view shown
- [ ] centre lines given
- [ ] all views labelled correctly
- [ ] border and title block

You must produce an isometric view and an exploded isometric view of the product. Remember, your product must have a minimum of three parts.

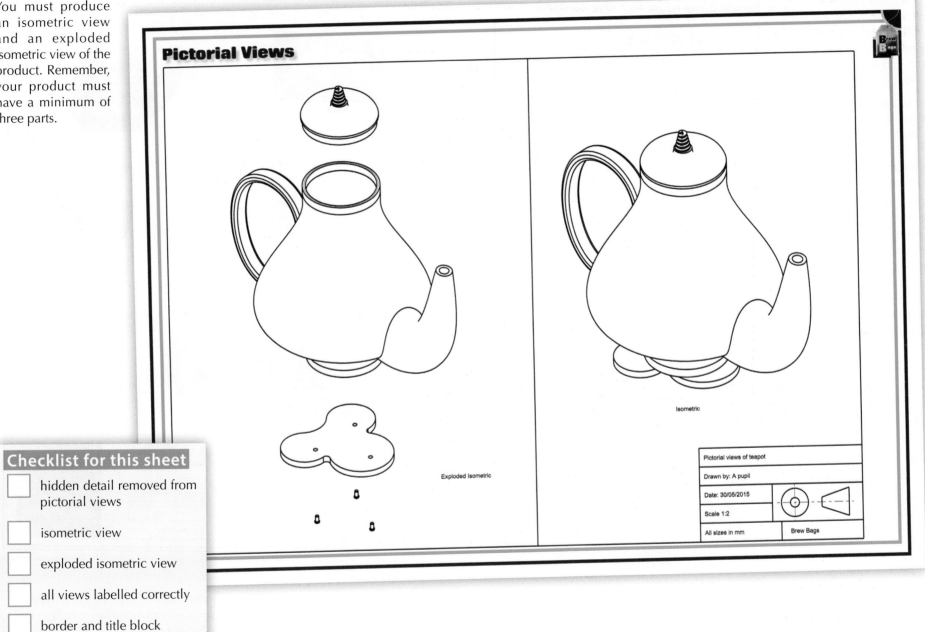

Pictorial Views

Exploded Isometric

Isometric

Pictorial views of teapot	
Drawn by: A pupil	
Date: 30/05/2015	
Scale 1:2	
All sizes in mm	Brew Bags

Checklist for this sheet

- [ ] hidden detail removed from pictorial views
- [ ] isometric view
- [ ] exploded isometric view
- [ ] all views labelled correctly
- [ ] border and title block

You must produce a modelling plan of how you created your product using the 3D modelling software.

You can produce this manually if you like, but it is far quicker to produce it using the computer.

This example uses screenshots of the different stages of development of the teapot, with short annotations to describe what has happened at each stage.

Modelling plan for the teapot

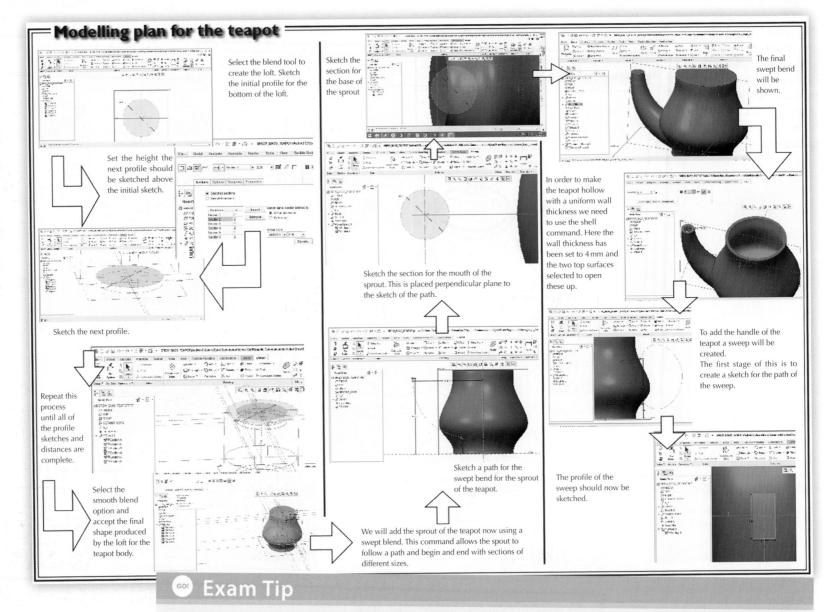

Select the blend tool to create the loft. Sketch the initial profile for the bottom of the loft.

Set the height the next profile should be sketched above the initial sketch.

Sketch the next profile.

Repeat this process until all of the profile sketches and distances are complete.

Select the smooth blend option and accept the final shape produced by the loft for the teapot body.

Sketch the section for the base of the sprout

Sketch the section for the mouth of the sprout. This is placed perpendicular plane to the sketch of the path.

Sketch a path for the swept bend for the sprout of the teapot.

We will add the sprout of the teapot now using a swept blend. This command allows the spout to follow a path and begin and end with sections of different sizes.

The final swept bend will be shown.

In order to make the teapot hollow with a uniform wall thickness we need to use the shell command. Here the wall thickness has been set to 4 mm and the two top surfaces selected to open these up.

To add the handle of the teapot a sweep will be created.
The first stage of this is to create a sketch for the path of the sweep.

The profile of the sweep should now be sketched.

Exam Tip

In your exam, you will be asked to produce a modelling plan to show how a product can be created using 3D CAD. You must use the key words described in this book to achieve marks for this. Use these terms and key words in the modelling plans you produce throughout the course to help you prepare for this type of question.

It is up to you whether you use a word processor for your modelling plan or whether you lay out the steps like a storyboard, as shown here.

Modelling plan for the teapot

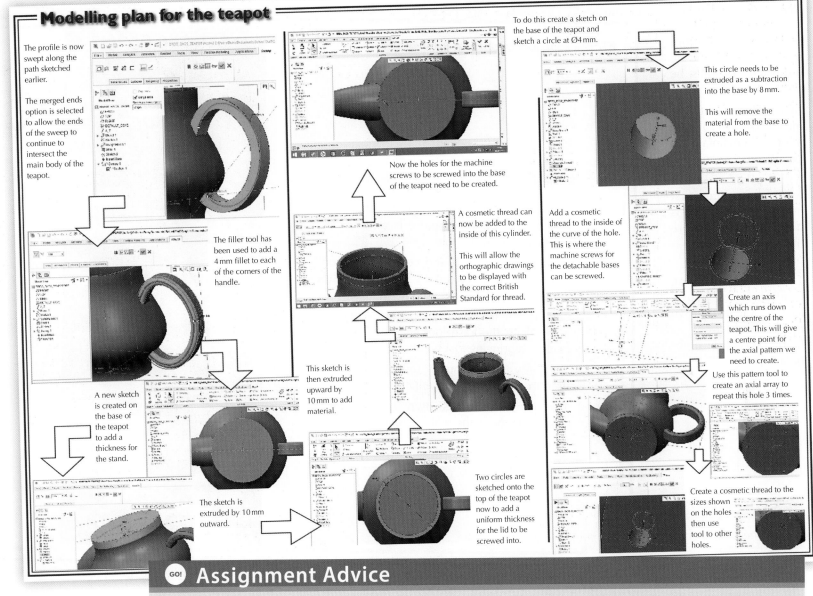

The profile is now swept along the path sketched earlier.

The merged ends option is selected to allow the ends of the sweep to continue to intersect the main body of the teapot.

The filler tool has been used to add a 4 mm fillet to each of the corners of the handle.

A new sketch is created on the base of the teapot to add a thickness for the stand.

The sketch is extruded by 10 mm outward.

Now the holes for the machine screws to be screwed into the base of the teapot need to be created.

This sketch is then extruded upward by 10 mm to add material.

Two circles are sketched onto the top of the teapot now to add a uniform thickness for the lid to be screwed into.

A cosmetic thread can now be added to the inside of this cylinder.

This will allow the orthographic drawings to be displayed with the correct British Standard for thread.

To do this create a sketch on the base of the teapot and sketch a circle at Ø4mm.

This circle needs to be extruded as a subtraction into the base by 8 mm.

This will remove the material from the base to create a hole.

Add a cosmetic thread to the inside of the curve of the hole. This is where the machine screws for the detachable bases can be screwed.

Create an axis which runs down the centre of the teapot. This will give a centre point for the axial pattern we need to create.

Use this pattern tool to create an axial array to repeat this hole 3 times.

Create a cosmetic thread to the sizes shown on the holes then use tool to other holes.

GO! **Assignment Advice**

When creating your 3D model, keep sketches on paper to help you create the different parts. This will help you get dimensions correct throughout the project. It will also help if you create some parts in context, using top-down modelling techniques to ensure the parts fit together.

Brew Bags asked for a final graphic of the roller banner presentation to be produced. This must be produced to scale.

Any DTP presentation must be shown to scale in order to maintain the correct proportions.

A smaller version would be printed first to check the client is happy with it before the final presentation is produced.

This saves printing consumables, such as ink, and expensive materials, such as fabric, acrylic or high-quality paper.

Final roller banner graphic

This layout meets the brief:

The image of the young women makes it obvious that the company is aiming the product at young people.

The Brew Bags logo and colours are used throughout the layout to emphasise the company identity or brand.

The use of text at angles creates impact and reflects the fresh look that this range of teapots is bringing to a traditional product.

The Brew Bags company font, Jagger SF, is used throughout the presentation.

The presentation shown is a scaled representation of the real-life roller banner.

Checklist for this sheet

- [ ] check all spelling is correct
- [ ] visual impact is excellent
- [ ] skilled use of design elements and design principles and DTP commands

Brew Bags – rendered environment

As part of the graphic proposal, Brew Bags specified that the teapot must be shown in a suitable environment. You must show material, light, reflections, shadows and texture in your environment. In the course assignment a decal must be included in the environment.

3D Rendered Environment

GO! Assignment Advice

You can use existing 3D models of items when creating your 3D environment. While the use of items from a CAD library is acceptable, you must ensure you reference where each of the parts has come from.

THE ASSESSMENT STANDARDS

171

This shows how each of the assessment standards is covered in the Brew Bags folio. Having a grid like this will make it easier for you and your teacher to keep a record of how you are progressing through the 2D and 3D Graphic Communication units of the course.

Brew Bags – preliminary graphics

These are the assessment standards that are covered by the preliminary graphics produced as part of this project.

If you meet these standards, then they can be recorded as passed.

The level of work required to pass each of the assessment standards is the equivalent of a C grade.

Preliminary graphics

1 Produce and interpret 2D orthographic sketches and drawings by:

1.1 Applying appropriate drawing standards, protocols and conventions to produce orthographic sketches of everyday objects, components and assemblies with dimensions and complex features.

3 Produce preliminary 2D designs and illustrations for a multi-page promotional document by:

3.1 Illustrating preliminary orthographic sketches of geometric forms and everyday objects.

3.2 Conducting preliminary research prior to the design of a promotional publication and preparing an outline specification.

3.3 Applying knowledge and understanding of graphic elements and principles to produce preliminary layout designs for a multi-page promotional document.

1 Produce and interpret pictorial sketches and drawings by:

1.1 Applying graphic communication skills to produce pictorial line sketches of everyday objects or buildings with complex features that demonstrate good proportion, line quality, and representation of the item.

3 Produce pictorial and 3D illustrations of everyday objects by:

3.1 Illustrating preliminary pictorial sketches or drawings of everyday objects, to interpret the light source, surface texture and materials.

4 Plan and produce promotional publications incorporating pictorial and/or 3D models by:

4.1 Designing a preliminary layout to incorporate a pictorial and/or 3D model to create relevant visual impact in response to a brief or theme.

4.2 Producing promotional publications to incorporate a pictorial and/or 3D model.

4.3 Evaluating the effectiveness of the format to its target audience in relation to design principles and elements.

Production graphics

1 Produce and interpret 2D orthographic sketches and drawings by:

1.2 Using graphic communication equipment accurately and effectively and applying appropriate drawing standards, protocols and conventions to produce projected 2D line drawings of everyday objects, components and assemblies with dimensions and complex features.

2 Produce 2D computer-aided designed production drawings by:

2.1 Applying computer-aided design skills, knowledge and understanding accurately and effectively and using appropriate drawing standards, protocols and conventions to create related orthographic views of single components and assemblies.

2.2 Applying computer-aided design skills, knowledge and understanding accurately and effectively and using appropriate drawing standards to create three examples of technical detail.

2.3 Applying computer-aided design skills accurately and effectively and using appropriate drawing standards to add textual and numerical information to orthographic computer-aided designed work.

1 Produce and interpret pictorial sketches and drawings by:

1.2 Applying graphic communication skills to produce pictorial line drawings of everyday objects or buildings with complex features that demonstrate accuracy in proportion, line quality, type and representation of the item.

2 Produce 3D computer-aided designed models and associated production drawings by:

2.1 Applying computer-aided design skills accurately and effectively and using appropriate assembly techniques to create 3D models of everyday objects with complex features and technical detail.

2.2 Describing and justifying 3D modelling techniques used to generate models of everyday objects with complex features.

2.3 Applying computer-aided design skills, knowledge and understanding accurately and effectively and using appropriate drawing standards to add textual and numerical information to pictorial computer-aided designed work.

Brew Bags – production graphics

Through the production graphics produced, you will meet each of the assessment standards shown.

These can be recorded on one sheet by the teacher in order to make a record of your progress. Organising it this way will keep the process as simple to understand and quick to complete as possible.

Brew Bags – promotional graphics

The assessment standards shown will be met through the work completed during this part of the project.

It is important to emphasise that these standards are not in place to make things difficult for you to pass the course, but to help you do so. They make clear what sort of drawings, sketches and graphic techniques should be learned and used throughout the course.

There are no marks awarded for the units – they are simply pass or fail. The minimum standard required to achieve the units and meet the assessment standards is equivalent to a grade C at Higher Graphic Communication.

Promotional graphics	
3 Produce preliminary 2D designs and illustrations for a multi-page promotional document by: 3.1 Illustrating preliminary orthographic sketches of geometric forms and everyday objects. 3.2 Conducting preliminary research prior to the design of a promotional publication and preparing an outline specification. 3.3 Applying knowledge and understanding of graphic elements and principles to produce preliminary layout designs for a multi-page promotional document. **4 Create a multi-page 2D promotional publication and a project set of promotional publications by:** 4.1 Using software accurately and effectively to construct a master page/template for a multi-page promotional publication. 4.2 Producing a multi-page promotional publication with complex features, which communicates effectively with its target audience and has relevant visual impact.	**3 Produce pictorial and 3D illustrations of everyday objects by:** 3.2 Creating a rendered 3D computer-aided designed model of a complex everyday object to interpret the light source, with tonal change, surface texture and materials. 3.3 Using computer-aided design software appropriately to create an environment or scene with relevant visual impact, applying surface texture and materials, to situate and effectively enhance a pictorial illustration.

Evaluation	
1 Produce and interpret 2D orthographic sketches and drawings by: 1.3 Describing and justifying the use of the main types of graphic communication employed in the design, manufacturing and marketing of a product. **4 Create a multi-page 2D promotional publication and a project set of promotional publications by:** 4.3 Describing and justifying the use of promotional graphics in industry and commerce and their impact on the environment and society.	**1 Produce and interpret pictorial sketches and drawings by:** 1.3 Describing and justifying the use of the main types of 3D and pictorial graphic communication employed in the design, manufacturing and marketing of a product. **4 Plan and produce promotional publications incorporating pictorial and/or 3D models by:** 4.4 Describing the purpose of 3D modelling in commercial/industrial settings, the impact on the environment and society.

Brew Bags – evaluation

The evaluation process occurs naturally throughout the process of producing the graphic response to the Brew Bags brief.

The assessment standards listed are covered throughout.

This completes the set of assessment standards required to pass both the 2D and 3D Graphic Communication units in order to pass the course.

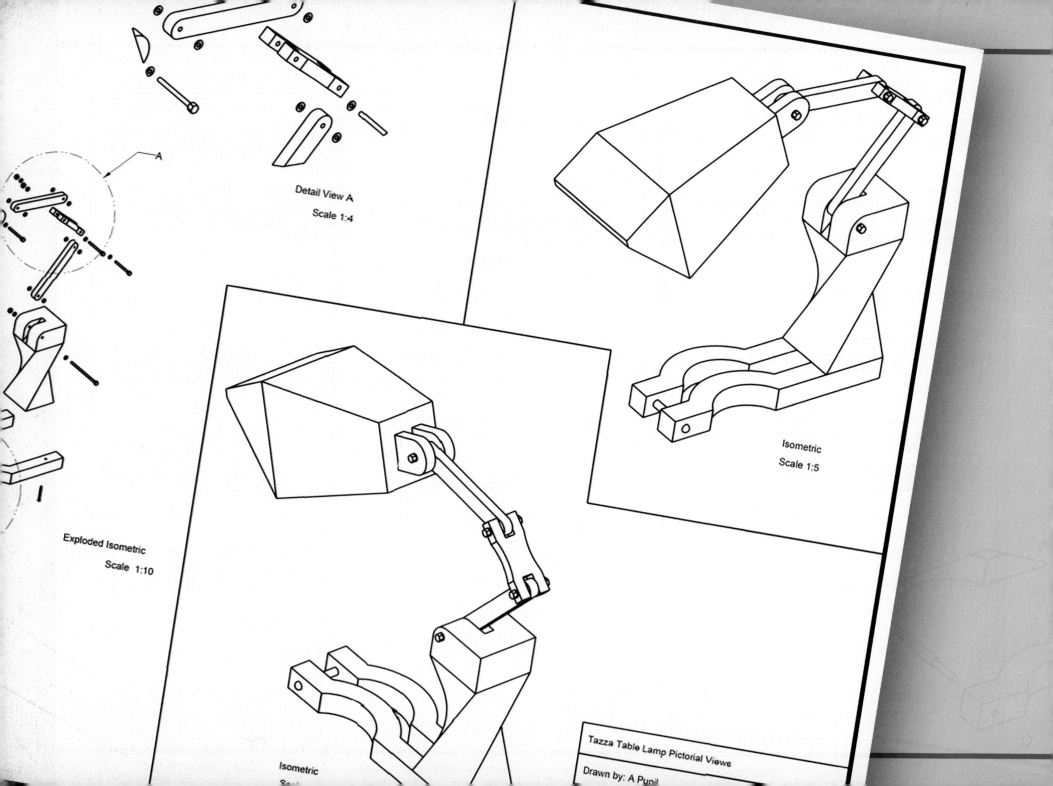

A

Detail View A

Scale 1:4

Exploded Isometric

Scale 1:10

Isometric

Scale 1:5

Isometric

Tazza Table Lamp Pictorial Views

Drawn by: A Pupil

Chapter 9

The Assignment

You will learn

- **The assignment – Tazza Lighting example**

The assignment – Tazza Lighting example

The final assignment is worth 50% of your overall mark for Higher Graphic Communication. It is marked out of 70 and is completed in an open book environment during class time and under teacher supervision. It is not permitted to complete any work for this at home or anywhere you are not supervised by your assessor.

You must complete no more than ten A3 pages when meeting the requirements of the assignment.

There are four areas that you must cover when completing the assignment. These are:

1. Analysis

2. Preliminary graphics

3. Production graphics

4. Promotional graphics

Unlike at National 5, you are not required to produce a sheet to cover the evaluation of the assignment. It is assumed that, by the time you reach this level, you will be continually evaluating your work throughout the graphic projects you complete. The evidence of this evaluation should be referred to throughout the assignment.

The assignment example shown here is not an official SQA assignment, but does show how you could structure your assignment in order to gain maximum marks.

Assignment task: Tazza Lighting

Your task is to create a graphic proposal for a company called Tazza Lighting, who are looking for a range of lighting that uses existing fixings as part of their range of industrial-themed furniture.

Tazza Lighting have a logo and a colour scheme, which must be visible throughout their advertising as they are building their company brand. The logo is included in your pack as a vector graphic file. The colours used are:

RGB code: R - 160; G - 0; B - 121

RGB code: R - 255; G - 255; B - 0

Some of the knock-down fittings that Tazza insist you use are available as step files, which are also included in your assignment pack.

Tazza Lighting also require an advert that will accompany the lamp on a shop display. This should be no larger than A3 in size and must be able to stand independently.

You must display the completed proposal in a suitable environment.

Your task is to **analyse** the graphical requirements for the graphic proposal and produce the **preliminary, production** and **promotional** graphics required to meet the brief.

Analysis

One of the most important parts of the analysis is to identify the specific types of drawing that need to be completed within the assignment. This is an easy place to pick up marks if you follow the advice given in the checklist below. You also need to identify the key points in the assignment specification.

GO! Assignment Advice

Ensure you list all of the drawings you need to create in order to complete the assignment.

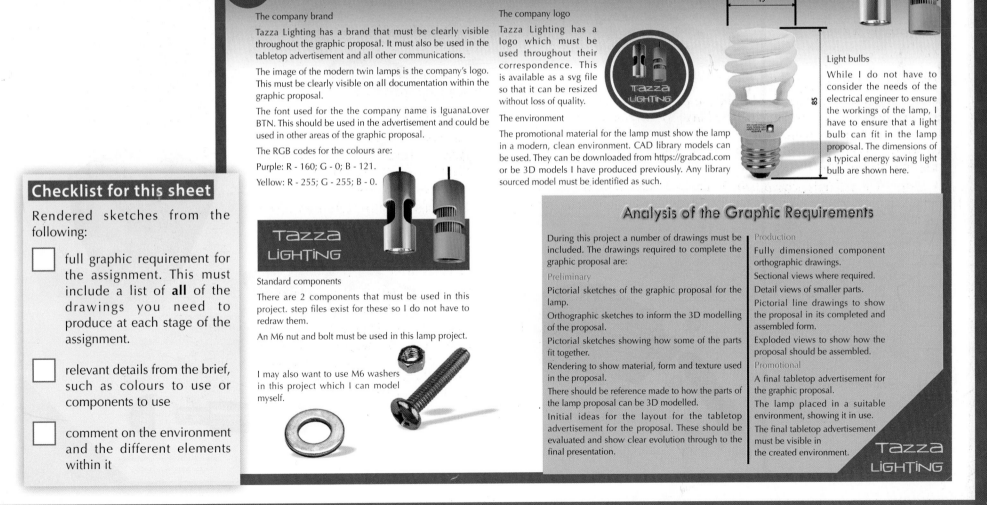

ANALYSIS

The company brand

Tazza Lighting has a brand that must be clearly visible throughout the graphic proposal. It must also be used in the tabletop advertisement and all other communications.

The image of the modern twin lamps is the company's logo. This must be clearly visible on all documentation within the graphic proposal.

The font used for the the company name is IguanaLover BTN. This should be used in the advertisement and could be used in other areas of the graphic proposal.

The RGB codes for the colours are:

Purple: R - 160; G - 0; B - 121.

Yellow: R - 255; G - 255; B - 0.

The company logo

Tazza Lighting has a logo which must be used throughout their correspondence. This is available as a svg file so that it can be resized without loss of quality.

The environment

The promotional material for the lamp must show the lamp in a modern, clean environment. CAD library models can be used. They can be downloaded from https://grabcad.com or be 3D models I have produced previously. Any library sourced model must be identified as such.

Light bulbs

While I do not have to consider the needs of the electrical engineer to ensure the workings of the lamp, I have to ensure that a light bulb can fit in the lamp proposal. The dimensions of a typical energy saving light bulb are shown here.

45

85

Standard components

There are 2 components that must be used in this project. step files exist for these so I do not have to redraw them.

An M6 nut and bolt must be used in this lamp project.

I may also want to use M6 washers in this project which I can model myself.

Analysis of the Graphic Requirements

During this project a number of drawings must be included. The drawings required to complete the graphic proposal are:

Preliminary

Pictorial sketches of the graphic proposal for the lamp.

Orthographic sketches to inform the 3D modelling of the proposal.

Pictorial sketches showing how some of the parts fit together.

Rendering to show material, form and texture used in the proposal.

There should be reference made to how the parts of the lamp proposal can be 3D modelled.

Initial ideas for the layout for the tabletop advertisement for the proposal. These should be evaluated and show clear evolution through to the final presentation.

Production

Fully dimensioned component orthographic drawings.

Sectional views where required.

Detail views of smaller parts.

Pictorial line drawings to show the proposal in its completed and assembled form.

Exploded views to show how the proposal should be assembled.

Promotional

A final tabletop advertisement for the graphic proposal.

The lamp placed in a suitable environment, showing it in use.

The final tabletop advertisement must be visible in the created environment.

Tazza LIGHTING

Checklist for this sheet

Rendered sketches from the following:

☐ full graphic requirement for the assignment. This must include a list of **all** of the drawings you need to produce at each stage of the assignment.

☐ relevant details from the brief, such as colours to use or components to use

☐ comment on the environment and the different elements within it

Preliminary – initial pictorial sketches

Preliminary sketches are used to give the client an idea of proposed solutions for their product. They should be rendered to a high quality to make them look realistic.

You are permitted to use electronic methods, such as a graphic sketching app, to produce these drawings.

GO! Assignment Advice

Think carefully about the forms you choose to create as they must contain enough complexity to be able to create 3D models that are difficult enough to receive full marks for that part of the assignment.

Checklist for this sheet

Sketches:

- [ ] isometric
- [ ] one-point perspective
- [ ] two-point perspective
- [ ] marker rendering
- [ ] pencil rendering
- [ ] 3D CAD model planning
- [ ] relevant dimensions

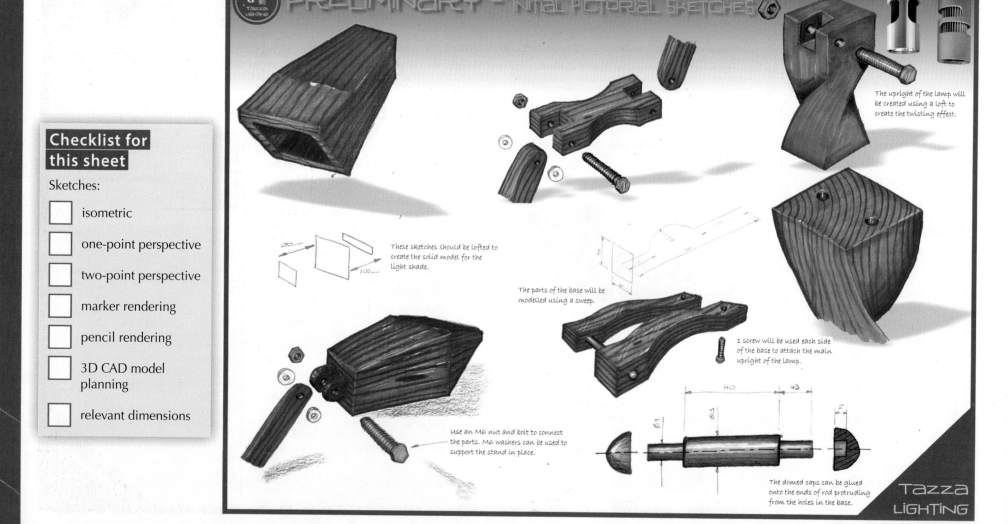

PRELIMINARY – initial pictorial sketches

The upright of the lamp will be created using a loft to create the twisting effect.

These sketches should be lofted to create the solid model for the light shade.

The parts of the base will be modelled using a sweep.

1 screw will be used each side of the base to attach the main upright of the lamp.

Use an M6 nut and bolt to connect the parts. M6 washers can be used to support the stand in place.

The domed caps can be glued onto the ends of rod protruding from the holes in the base.

Tazza Lighting

Preliminary – orthographic sketches

Orthographic sketches should then be developed to allow 3D CAD models of the components to be produced. You must provide enough dimensions on your preliminary orthographic sketches that will allow the components to be fully modeled using 3D CAD software. You should also show enlarged views and sectional views if necessary.

GO! Assignment Advice

To get full marks here, you must provide all the dimensions required to be able to create a 3D model of the product. You must also follow all British Standards when dimensioning and sketching these drawings.

Checklist for this sheet

- [ ] orthographic component views of each of the parts of the proposal
- [ ] all dimensions required to create the 3D CAD model
- [ ] dimensions follow British Standards 8888
- [ ] all centre lines shown
- [ ] hidden detail, hatching lines shown

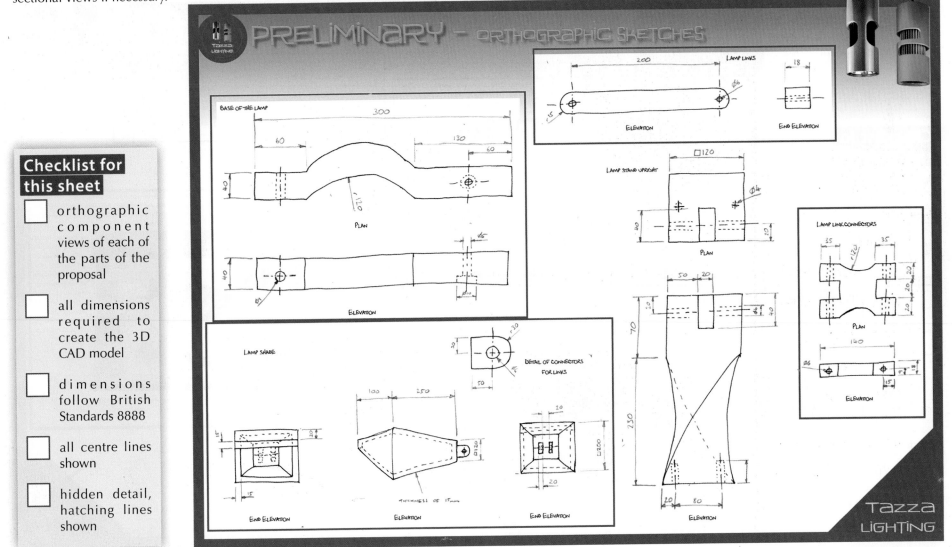

Preliminary – DTP planning

The DTP work must be planned in order to create a display with effective visual impact. When producing layouts and evaluating them, you must use the correct terms associated with the design elements, design principles and DTP features.

It is a good idea to produce these plans using DTP software. This makes the process more efficient.

GO! Assignment Advice

Use DTP software to plan your layouts. Save the various stages of evolution as different versions and show each version on this sheet. Comment at each stage, ensuring that you explain why you have chosen to make changes. Use the correct terms for the design elements, design principles and DTP work.

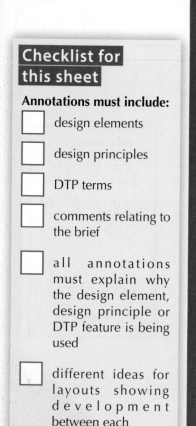

Checklist for this sheet

Annotations must include:

- [ ] design elements
- [ ] design principles
- [ ] DTP terms
- [ ] comments relating to the brief
- [ ] all annotations must explain why the design element, design principle or DTP feature is being used
- [ ] different ideas for layouts showing development between each

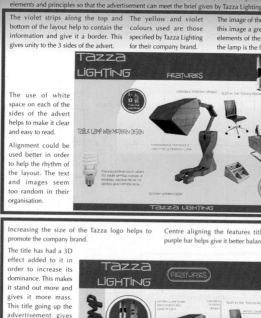

PRELIMINARY – TABLETOP ADVERTISEMENT DEVELOPMENT

The tabletop advert must be no larger than A3 in size. Thumbnails and layouts were produced and evaluated against the design elements and principles so that the advertisement can meet the brief given by Tazza Lighting.

Sources for images:
Wooden office chair - http://img.sahmone.net/images/office-turn.com/wpcontent/uploads/2011/10/Bentley WengeSleek-Wood-Office-Chairs.jpg
Wooden file organiser: http://g02.a.alicdn.com/ki/HTB1nhZjIXXXXcxXXXXq6xXFXXXMDeli- 9842 Wooden-Stationery- Holder-School-and-font-b-Office-b-font-Sup- plies-fontb-File.jpg

Wooden desk tidy - http://bleistift.memm .de/wpcontent/uplo ads/2011/02/ desktop butler -empty.jpg
Light bulb - https://d31wx ntiwn0x96.cloudfront.net/ cmtetr/productimages /70. jpg ?width 4 00&height=400 &etag=%2237c684d7e95fc 11ce93b62b2409041a7%22

Wooden office desk http://k umfree.com/wpcontent/up loads/ravishinguniquewoodendesk-featmodernpersonal-computerandaluminum-tableleg-forcoolofficedesksschemecoolofficedesksfurniture-excitingchoice-cool-officedesks-d.jpg

Stage 1

The violet strips along the top and bottom of the layout help to contain the information and give it a border. This gives unity to the 3 sides of the advert.

The yellow and violet colours used are those specified by Tazza Lighting for their company brand.

The image of the lamp dominates the advert. Giving this image a greater proportion than the rest of the elements of the presentation makes it obvious that the lamp is the focus of the advertisement.

The use of white space on each of the sides of the advert helps to make it clear and easy to read.

Alignment could be used better in order to help the rhythm of the layout. The text and images seem too random in their organisation.

The yellow flashbar helps to make the lamp appear to come toward the viewer. It also gives the layout unity as it runs through each of the 3 sides of the advert.

Stage 2

The two words of the company name have been right aligned and have also been right aligned with the fold of the advert.

An emboss has been added to the features title and border in order to make it contrast with the Tazza Lighting text. This features title could be moved to the centre of the top bar of colour to give better balance to this.

The Tazza Lighting logo has been made larger in order to give it more dominance. Having it positioned in close proximity to the title of the advert helps make it obvious they belong together.

The title of the advert has also been turned to be read upward in order to make it contrast with the rest of the advert.

It may be better to use lines in order to visually attach the text labels to the parts of the lamp being described. Lines and text could also be used to make the range of Tazza products more clear.

Increasing the size of the Tazza logo helps to promote the company brand.

The title has had a 3D effect added to it in order to increase its dominance. This makes it stand out more and gives it more mass. This title going up the advertisement gives this side of the advert excellent balance.

The contrast of the purple text on the yellow background helps the title stand out.

Placing a white halo around the light bulb gives the feeling of light for this part of the advertisement.

Centre aligning the features title and the purple bar helps give it better balance.

The lines added to the labels for the various products add unity between the labels and images. Using this method to label the image of the lamp aids the unity of these labels.

The title of the advert has been enlarged in order to give it dominance. The larger proportion of it allows it to stand out.

A drop shadow could be added to the lamp in order to make it come forward and toward the viewer.

Final Stage

The text describing the lamp is left aligned with the yellow background on the left of the advertisement.

The drop shadow added to the lamp adds depth to bring it off the page.

Tazza LIGHTING

THE ASSIGNMENT

Production drawings – component orthographics

All of the production drawings you complete have to have a border and title block. The details that should be included are described earlier in this book. Ensure that your sheets are clearly laid out. A good method is to draw lines between each of the different sets of component orthographic views.

The component production orthographic drawings must contain enough information to enable each of the parts to be manufactured. Ensure that all hidden detail, centre lines and dimensions are shown and that British Standards are followed throughout.

GO! Assignment Advice

Include enlarged detail views to show smaller parts clearly. Fully dimension each component and show all centre lines. You must ensure that you show all of the dimensions that would be required to manufacture the product.

Checklist for this sheet

Annotations must include:

- [ ] component orthographic views of all parts
- [ ] all centre lines shown
- [ ] Show all dimensions that would be required to be able to manufacture the parts shown
- [ ] hidden detail shown
- [ ] title block and border with lines separating views
- [ ] British Standards followed

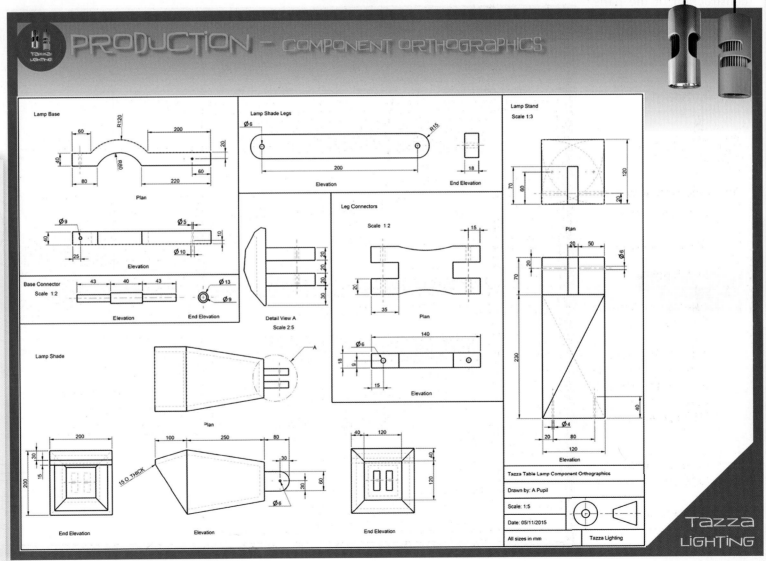

THE ASSIGNMENT

Production drawings – technical detail

Technical detail includes sectional views, enlarged detail views or exploded views. These types of drawing are needed to make it obvious how particular parts of a product are assembled or to show the internal construction of the parts.

You need to show at least one stepped sectional view.

GO! **Assignment Advice**

This sheet must contain an enlarged view and a sectional view. It is beneficial to include a stepped sectional view and a pictorial sectional view if it helps to understand any of the details. Orthographic or pictorial exploded views will help show how the product is assembled and are useful to include.

Checklist for this sheet

- [ ] full sectional view
- [ ] stepped sectional view
- [ ] enlarged detail view
- [ ] exploded view to show how parts are assembled
- [ ] all drawing labels are correct

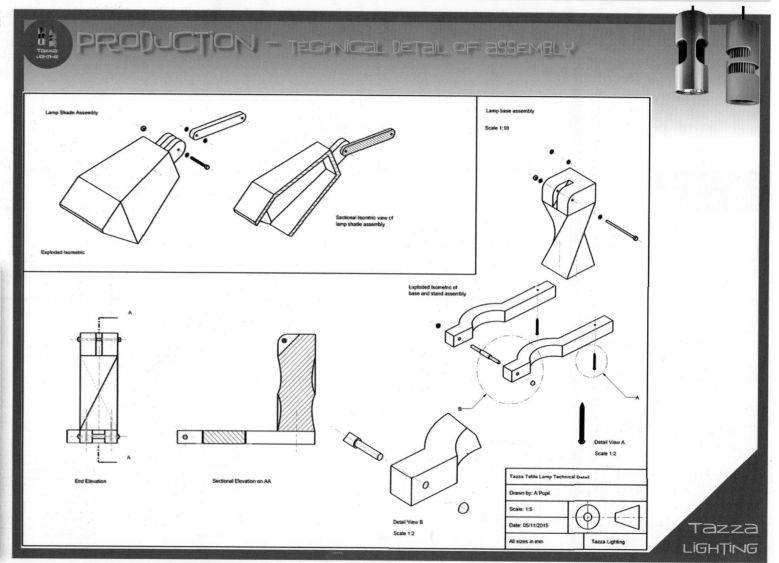

PRODUCTION – TECHNICAL DETAIL OF ASSEMBLY

Lamp Shade Assembly

Sectional Isometric view of lamp shade assembly

Exploded Isometric

Lamp base assembly

Scale 1:10

Exploded Isometric of base and stand assembly

End Elevation

Sectional Elevation on AA

Detail View B

Scale 1:2

Detail View A

Scale 1:2

Tazza Table Lamp Technical Detail

Drawn by: A Pupil

Scale: 1:5

Date: 05/11/2015

All sizes in mm

Tazza Lighting

Tazza LIGHTING

THE ASSIGNMENT

182

Production drawings – pictorial views

You have to show pictorial views of the assembled model. You must also include exploded pictorial views on this sheet to show how the model is put together.

GO! **Assignment Advice**

You must show an assembled and an exploded pictorial view on this sheet. You can also show pictorial enlarged detail views if suitable. Show a pictorial view from different sides if it will make the object clearer.

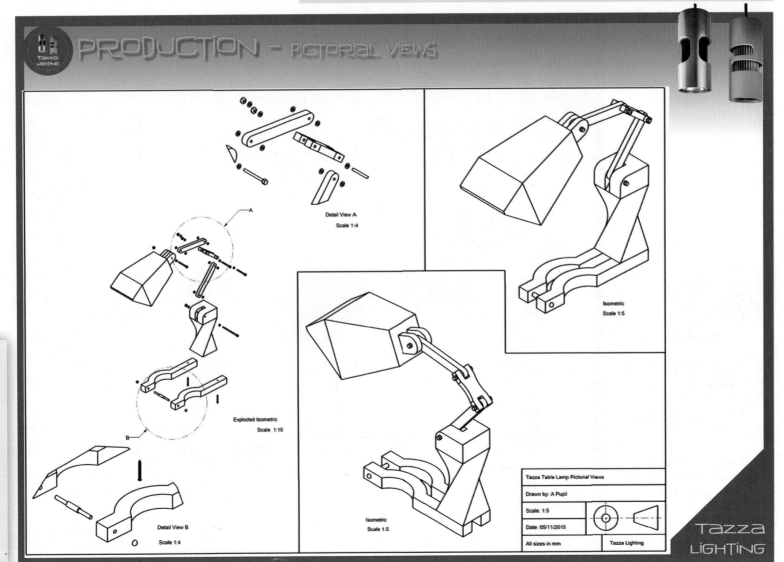

PRODUCTION – PICTORIAL VIEWS

Detail View A
Scale 1:4

Exploded Isometric
Scale 1:10

Detail View B
Scale 1:4

Isometric
Scale 1:5

Isometric
Scale 1:5

Tazza Table Lamp Pictorial Views	
Drawn by: A Pupil	
Scale: 1:5	
Date: 05/11/2015	
All sizes in mm	Tazza Lighting

Tazza LIGHTING

Checklist for this sheet

- [ ] isometric views
- [ ] exploded isometric view
- [ ] enlarged detail views of small parts
- [ ] each view must be labelled correctly

Promotional drawings – DTP work

A full-size version of the DTP work developed earlier in the assignment should be shown. It must show evidence of effective use of the design elements and the design principles. This image must be used within the environment.

GO! ## Assignment Advice

The DTP presentation must make excellent use of the design elements and design principles. Ensure you have a good knowledge of these so that you can apply them with skill. Study existing layouts to help generate ideas.

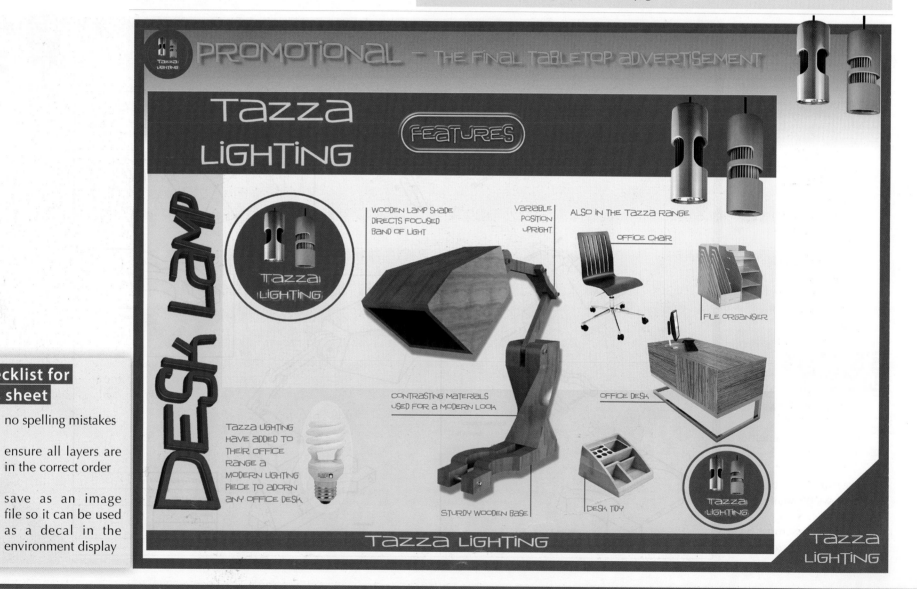

Checklist for this sheet

- [ ] no spelling mistakes
- [ ] ensure all layers are in the correct order
- [x] save as an image file so it can be used as a decal in the environment display

Promotional drawings – the environment

The environment will be assembled in 3D CAD and then rendered using specialist software. It must show the completed item in a relevant scene and include the DTP produced item as a decal.

GO! Assignment Advice

TThe environment should include the DTP produced item. It can also include CAD library parts that you have downloaded. Using specialist rendering software, such as Showcase® or KeyShot® will give the best results.

Checklist for this sheet

- [ ] show a close-up of the finished, rendered 3D model that you have produced preliminary, production and promotional graphics for

- [ ] ensure you show the DTP item you produced, displayed as a decal in the environment

- [ ] include at least two light sources in your rendered environment

- [ ] ensure you show materials, textures, shadows and reflections in your rendered scene

UZZ SPORT
YDRATES AND
WERS YOU BETTER THAN WATER

HERE AT BUZZ SPORT, WE KNOW THAT POWER DOESN'T COME FROM DETERMINATION ALONE. PEP TALKS AND MOTIVATIONAL SPEECHES CAN ONLY GO SO FAR.
WHY NOT TRUST THE EXPERTS AT BUZZ SPORT AND TRY OUR NEW SPORTS DRINK THAT HAS BEEN SCIENTIFICALLY PROVEN TO PROVIDE MORE POWER THAN ANY OTHER COMPETING PRODUCT? POWER, STRENGTH ANDD ENDURANCE CAN INCREASE BY OVER 25% - IT'S A FACT! GRAB A BOTTLE AND SEE THE RESULTS FOR YOURSELF.

DO YOU HAVE THE POWER?

#IHAVETHEPOWER

Chapter 10

Exam Questions

You will learn

- **The exam**
- **Digital advertising**
- **DTP printing techniques**
- **DTP - types of images**
- **The 3 Ps**

The exam for the course is worth 50% of your total mark.

Throughout this book there are helpful hints for you to follow so that you can successfully answer the exam questions and gain an excellent mark.

This part of the book will provide some help on how to structure your answers to typical exam questions.

3D CAD questions will definitely be a key feature of the exam. They will ask you to describe the process of creating extrudes and revolves.

In particular, at Higher level, you will be asked to describe how to carry out the following 3D CAD functions: extruding along a path, lofting and creating a helix.

Make sure you use the key words described in the 3D CAD section of this book. These are highlighted in bold in the exemplar answers shown here. It is also a good idea to use sketches to support your answer. These do not have to be works of art, but must clearly indicate what you describe in your answer.

3D CAD exam questions

A fashion company is looking to launch a range of new fragrances to compliment its clothes. Drawings for a bottle for the fragrance have been developed and now have to be created in CAD.

Describe how the CAD technician could create a 3D CAD model of the fragrance bottle. You may use sketches to support your answer.

GO! Exam Tip

When answering 3D CAD modeling questions you must make reference to some keywords. In this example these have been highlighted in bold. Underlining them in your exam will help you ensure you use these words.

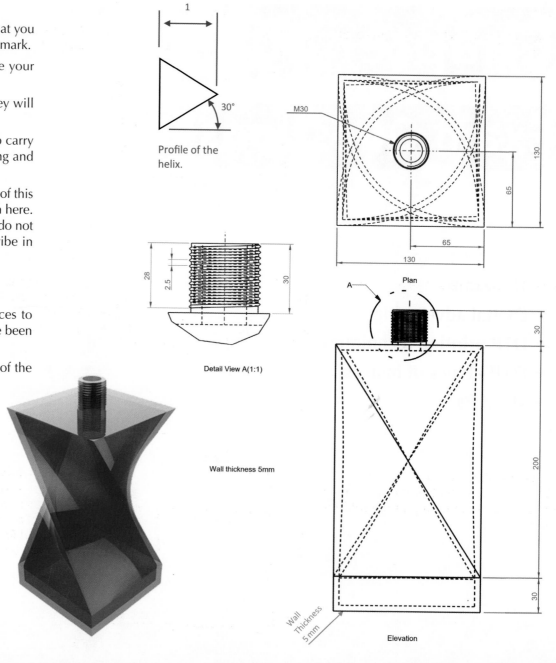

Profile of the helix.

Detail View A(1:1)

Wall thickness 5mm

Plan

Elevation

EXAM QUESTIONS

Step 1 – profile

Sketch the **profile** of the base of the bottle.

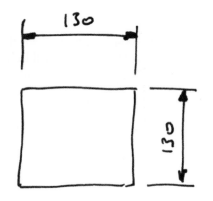

Step 2 – extrude

Extrude this profile by 30 mm.

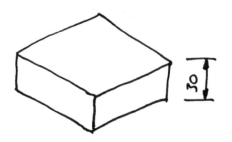

Step 3 – loft, profile

To create the **loft** for the bottle, two sketches are needed. First sketch a profile of 130 × 130 mm on top of the sold for the base.

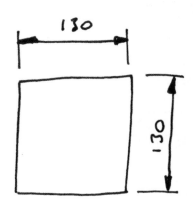

Step 4 – workplane

Create a new **workplane** 200 mm above the top of the sketch just drawn.

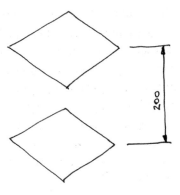

Step 5 – profile

Sketch the **profile** of the top of the bottle on this new workplane. This should be positioned directly above the original sketch.

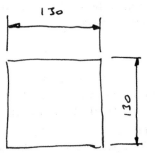

Step 6 – loft, loft path

Create a **loft** between the two sketches. This **loft** must contain a twist, so identify the **loft path** starting at one point on the bottom sketch and finish at the next point on the top sketch.

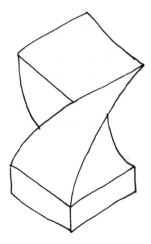

Step 7 – profile

For the top of the bottle, create a **profile** by sketching on the top face of the solid.

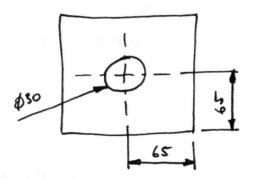

Step 8 – extrude

Extrude this profile upward by 30 mm.

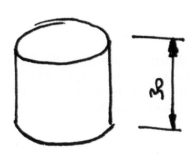

Step 9 – shell

Shell the solid to give a wall thickness of 5 mm. Select the top face of the bottle and open this.

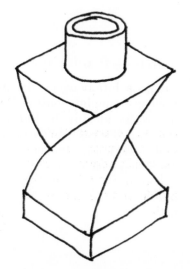

Step 10 – workplane

Create a **workplane** that passes through the centre of the bottle. This will be positioned 65 mm from the side of the bottle.

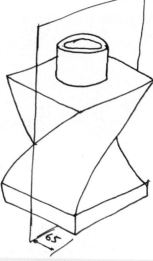

Step 11 – profile, helix, centre axis

Onto this workplane sketch the **profile** of the **helix**. Included in this sketch will be the **centre axis** and the offset distance. It is a good idea to label the profile and centre axis for clarity.

Step 12 – helix, pitch, length of axis

Use the **helix** command to create the helix. Define the **pitch** to be 2.5 mm. The **length of the helix** should be 28 mm.

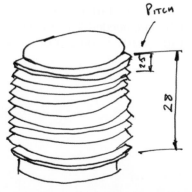

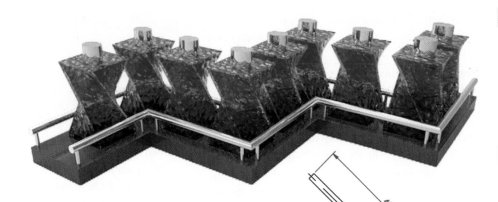

The perfume bottle is shown as it would be displayed on its display rack in a shop.

The rack is to be modelled using 3D CAD. Describe how the CAD technician would produce the rail of the rack.

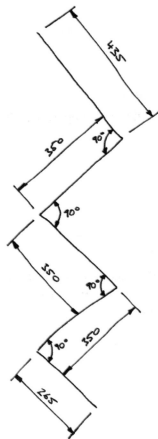

Step 1 – profile

Create a sketch of the **profile** of the rail.

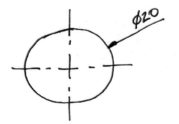

Step 2 – path, extrude along a path

On a separate sketch create the **path** for the solid to be created using the **extrude along a path** command.

Step 3 – extrude along a path, profile, path

Use the **extrude along a path** command to create the model, adding material. Select the circle as the **profile** and the line as the **path**.

Plan

DTP questions

It is possible to prepare for questions based on desktop publishing, even though the example used in the exam will change from paper to paper.

The most important thing is to know the design elements and design principles for a DTP document. You must mention these in your answers and explain how they have been used to assist the appearance of the publication.

There are a number of common features to look out for within any presentation.

The Design Elements

line

mass/weight

shape

size

texture

colour

The Design Principles

balance

contrast

alignment

proportion

rhythm

dominance

white space

emphasis

proximity/unity

grid structure

Colour is the most basic design element, so try to comment on the reasons for the colour choice. Refer to the properties of the colour and the feelings and emotions that are associated with it. If accent colours are used, it is normally to provide unity and rhythm.

Alignment is often used to help with rhythm so look for this and comment on it.

White space does not have to be areas of white – it can be areas of colour without any text or images.

Large parts of the layout can use proportion to create emphasis. Drop shadows are also often used to create emphasis.

Make sure you name the design element or design principle that you are referring to in each part of your answer.

The question will ask you to answer it according to the design elements and design principles, so in order to gain the marks you must mention them in your answer. A good tip here is to start each point by stating the design element or design principle you are describing.

Your exam is positively marked, which means that if the question is asking for five points (for 5 marks) and you make more than five points, you will not lose marks. You can make as many references to design elements and design principles as you like so, if you are unsure about an answer, make as many points as you can.

You can see in the exemplar exam question on the right, that many more points have been made than the 6 marks available require. You will not have correct answers cancelled out by wrong ones by answering questions in this way.

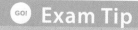

Exam Tip

Use the space at the end of the exam paper to list the design elements and design principles. Do this at the beginning of the exam while they are fresh in your memory. This is also a useful technique to help you settle your nerves in the exam. Then use these terms in each point you make in your answer.

Exam Tip

DTP publications often use the design elements and design principles in similar ways. Prepare answers for common uses to help you answer the questions in the exam.

Describe how the advertisement on the right has used the design elements and design principles to convey the key information about the product being advertised.

(6 marks)

Shape – a rectangle has been used to create a border for the text and images. This forms a frame to contain all of the images and body text on the poster and keep them together.

Colour – accent colours have been used throughout the poster. These colours have been picked from the bottle. This helps with the rhythm of the poster as it is obvious that the various parts belong together.

Colour – the lighter tone of green used around the man helps to make this part of the poster dominant. The gradient fill becoming darker toward the outside gives good rhythm to the advertisement, guiding the reader's eye from the dominant image to the edges of the poster.

Mass/weight – the image of the man has greater mass than the area of text on the left. This gives balance to the advertisement and means the lengthy area of text is more likely to be read.

Contrast – the green, pink and white contrast so that the text stands out against the background. The white text contrasts with the dark background to give it emphasis. The title is placed on a pink background to create contrast with the rest of the poster to help it stand out.

Contrast – reverse text is used for the title and subtitles to make them stand out from the body text. Drop shadows have been applied to these titles and subtitles to create further emphasis.

Contrast – the white line and background for the text on the bottom-right of the poster contrast with the bottle. The bottle being placed in front of this area helps it to come forward from the poster. The white rectangle here acts as a flashbar.

Alignment – the body text, heading and the tagline are left aligned with each other. This helps with the rhythm of the text, guiding the reader from one part down to the next.

Proportion – the large image dominates the poster. As the next largest items, the titles are then read, which leads you onto the smaller body text creating **rhythm**. As the bottle is also large in size, it is quickly noticed by the reader.

Proximity/unity - the bottle being positioned close to the large image makes this the focal point of the poster. It is obvious that this is the product being advertised.

White space – the areas to the left of the poster are left clear so that the poster is not too crowded and to allow the reader breathing space. It helps to give the main parts of the poster visual impact.

Digital advertising

You are likely to be asked questions about digital methods of advertising. These questions will ask you about the advantages of using this method of advertising for the consumer and the producer and also their environmental impact.

You must not answer these questions with 'it is easier' or 'it is quicker'. You must quantify these answers and state exactly what is easier or quicker.

Some advantages for the consumer include:

- One device can be used to view a large number of magazines/publications, which can increase the target market.
- The user can view these digital publications over a range of devices, even when it is dark.
- Website links can be embedded into the articles and the user can click on them while reading the article. These links can help increase immediate or impulse sales at any time of the day.
- The user does not have to go to a shop to buy a magazine, as they can download it to their device.
- The magazines can also be lower in cost, as the publisher does not have to cover costs associated with printing.
- Articles can include embedded videos. This can create more interest and allow the user to better understand sections of the article.
- The publications can be converted into different languages and read on one device.
- It is easy to zoom into small details in an image or make small text sizes easier to read.
- Many people use social networks and will share articles they find interesting using these platforms. This can increase the potential audience for adverts within articles.
- The digital format can also be copied and pasted onto social networks to reach a larger audience.

There are also advantages for the advertising company. These include:

- Newspapers and magazines will publish targeted articles through social media. Their advertising revenue can increase due to a greater number of viewers.
- An advertising space on a digital publication can be made from a slideshow. This can show a greater range of adverts and products in a small space to increase advertising revenue. The moving slideshow images can also be more eye catching to the reader and encourage further exploration of the products.
- Videos displaying a product being used can be embedded into adverts.
- As these adverts are often linked to the websites of the company selling the product, people can instantly make purchases or carry out further research into the product.
- The pricing for these products is real time, to appeal to consumers and be up to date.
- Changes can be made to adverts immediately without the need for reprinting.
- It is better for the environment because printing costs, materials and fuel are saved.

Some disadvantages of digital advertising are:

- Printing companies can struggle to survive, causing job losses in this industry.
- Openly shared digital information can be easy to copy, which creates copyright issues.
- Only people with digital devices can view digital adverts, which can reduce the potential market for the publication.
- Digital publications can only be viewed where there is access to the Internet.
- Many users prefer paper copies to read from.
- Paper copies can be left for a range of people to access them, for example, in waiting rooms or on passenger aircraft.

GO! Exam Tip

Learn 3 points from each of these areas to help you answer this type of question. Ensure that you quantify your answers and relate them to the exam question being asked.

DTP printing techniques

It is likely that you will be asked to demonstrate your understanding of DTP pre-press and printing techniques. Within this, you may be asked about registration marks, crop marks and image types.

Registration marks allow the accuracy of the printing alignment of the CMYK colours to be checked. This is an important part of the printing process to prevent expensive print runs with mistakes. If the printing heads are not aligned correctly, then images will appear blurry.

These are two examples of registration marks that can be used.

Crop marks show where the pages are trimmed by machine in order to cut the pages of a publication to the required size. These are particularly helpful when there are bleed images. Any images or part of a presentation that are to extend to the edges of the page will have to be printed beyond these crop marks to ensure accuracy when trimmed.

DTP – types of images

There are a range of image types that can be used when producing a DTP document. You will be required to demonstrate an understanding of these in your exam.

Image types are an important consideration. Vector files will predominantly be used when an image might need to be resized without loss of quality. Solid colour fills within vector images can be easily edited within DTP software – these simple changes do not require photo editing software.

Raster or bitmap images will be used when the image needs to be edited in more detail in the production of layouts. A simple raster or bitmap image will have smaller file sizes than a vector file of a complex image. This makes raster images ideal for being used in web-based presentations. Sometimes the quality of this type of image can be unsuitable for large print runs, especially if the image has been enlarged and become pixelated.

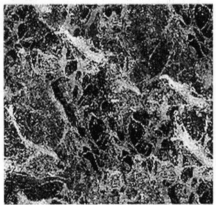

Two images are shown here. The image on the right is far more complex than the one on the left. If both of these images were vector files then the image on the right would have a much larger file size than that of the image on the left. In contrast to this, if these were raster or bitmap images, they would have the same file size. This is why raster files tend to be used to display images on the Internet.

EXAM QUESTIONS

The 3 Ps

You may be asked about the types of drawing produced in the 3 Ps. It can be advantageous to learn some small phrases that you can use to answer such questions.

Preliminary

These are initial sketches that give the client an idea of what the graphic proposal will look like. Preliminary drawings can be produced using either manual or digital techniques.

They will also be used to inform the development of the CAD drawings.

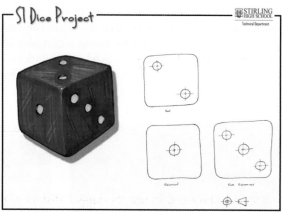

Production

These are high-quality, CAD produced, fully-dimensioned drawings that will allow manufacture. These can include: sectional views, enlarged views, cutaway views, exploded views, assemblies and component views.

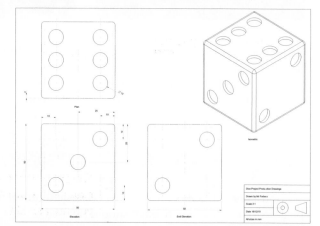

Promotional

These are computer produced, fully rendered images that will advertise the product. These often show the product in context for consumers and will contain some advertising material produced using DTP methods.

GO! Exam Tip

Preparing answers for this type of question before the day of the exam can help you gain easy marks.

Tolerances

Often a question about tolerances is asked in a similar way to the method shown here. It is common for you to be tested on your knowledge of the range of methods of tolerancing and your ability to work out the range of dimensions based upon a drawing.

A fence post and gate post are shown in the drawing below.

State the minimum and maximum size X is allowed to be.

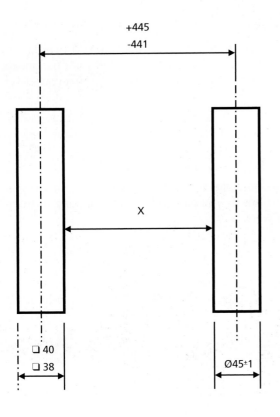

Minimum size for X

To find this you need to use the smallest distance between the centres of the two posts. Follow this by finding the largest possible widths for the posts. You must remember to halve the widths of the posts.

$$441 - 20 - 23 = \underline{398}$$

Maximum size for X

To find this you need to use the largest distance between the centres of the two posts. Follow this by finding the smallest possible widths of the posts. You must remember to halve the widths of the posts.

$$445 - 19 - 22 = \underline{404}$$

 Exam Tip

You should take a calculator into your exam to ensure no mistakes are made if you are asked to carry out calculations.

Architectural drawings

You may be asked about some of the details found in the drawings used when developing land and buildings. It is important to note that you should never duplicate an answer for more than one type of drawing.

Floor Plans – scale 1:50

- north symbol
- material contained within walls, such as insulation or brickwork
- plumbing and electrical fittings
- furniture and flooring layout
- building features, such as stairs, windows, doors, garage doors

Site Plans – scale 1:200

- the size and position of a building and its boundary area to scale
- the north symbol, to show the direction that the building and other features are facing
- contour lines
- trees shown in position
- the position of drainage and amenities, such as gas, electrical and water supplies

Location Plans – scale 1:1250

- north symbol, to allow the plan to be read properly in relation to a map
- the size of a building and surrounding area to scale
- location of building and surrounding streets and buildings
- any geographical details that would be found on an OS map, such as contour lines, rivers, woodland, footpaths, railways, bridges, lakes, etc.

CAD library

You should memorise a short passage in order to answer questions on what a CAD library or a library of stock CAD models is and why they are used.

You can use a phrase similar to the one below:

A CAD library is a collection of commonly used components, which can be placed in a drawing without the need for redrawing them each time. This saves the CAD technician time when producing drawings.

CAD libraries can be used to store 3D CAD models (which can be used within projects) or to store building symbols for use in architectural drawings.

Revision for your exam

You must set aside enough time for revision while still maintaining a healthy lifestyle. Exercise can help you relax and retain more information. You must take regular breaks from work to rest your brain. Remember that your brain is a muscle and needs time to recover from long periods of exertion.

Ensure you get plenty of sleep before your exam by going to bed early. Do not leave your revision until the last minute as this is very stressful. Begin your revision program five months before the final exam.

The best way to be as relaxed and confident as possible for your exam is to ensure you are as prepared as possible. Study this book throughout the year, answer as many past paper questions as you can and use the marking instructions to help you structure your answers.

Good luck!

GO! Exam Tip

Learn the scales of these drawings and at least 3 different features included in them.

Revision Notes

You should use this space throughout the year to record any notes that will help you revise for your exam.

ISBN 9780007549337

Published by
Leckie & Leckie Ltd
An imprint of HarperCollins*Publishers*
Westerhill Road, Bishopbriggs, Glasgow,
G64 2QT
T: 0844 576 8126   F: 0844 576 8131
leckieandleckie@harpercollins.co.uk
www.leckieandleckie.co.uk

Commissioning Editors: Fiona Burns and Katherine Wilkinson
Managing Editor: Craig Balfour

Special thanks to
Jill Laidlaw (copyedit)
Rebecca Skinner (editorial and proofread)
Louise Robb (proofread)
Keren McGill (proofread)
Lauren Reid (editorial)
Ken Vail (design and layout)

Printed in Great Britain by Martins the Printers

A CIP Catalogue record for this book is available from the British Library.

Acknowledgements

P11 (br) © dboystudio / Shutterstock, Inc; P20 © NORBERT MILLAUER / Staff / Getty Images; P21 (bl) © Alexander Scharnweber / Alamy Stock Photo; P21 (br) © Alpha and Omega Collection / Alamy Stock Photo; P22 (tl) © Hugh Threlfall / Alamy Stock Photo; P22 (bl) © Shamleen / Shutterstock, Inc; P25 (bl) © Alexey Boldin / Shutterstock, Inc; P25 One Drive App © Daniel Krason / Shutterstock, Inc; P25 Dropbox App © iJeab / Shutterstock, Inc; P25 Google Drive App © Maxx Satori / Shutterstock, Inc; P29 (tr) © Diabluses / Shutterstock, Inc; P31 (bl) © Phanie / Alamy Stock Photo; P32 (t) © HarperCollins Publishers; P32 (b) Cultura Creative (RF) / Alamy Stock Photo; P70 sketches Copyright © Scottish Qualifications Authority; P71 sketches Copyright © Scottish Qualifications Authority

Sketches and drawings by Barry Forbes

All other images © Shutterstock.com

Whilst every effort has been made to trace the copyright holders, in cases where this has been unsuccessful, or if any have inadvertently been overlooked, the Publishers would gladly receive any information enabling them to rectify any error or omission at the first opportunity.

MIX
Paper from responsible sources
FSC
www.fsc.org   FSC® C007454

FSC™ is a non-profit international organisation established to promote the responsible management of the world's forests. Products carrying the FSC label are independently certified to assure consumers that they come from forests that are managed to meet the social, economic and ecological needs of present and future generations, and other controlled sources.

Find out more about HarperCollins and the environment at
www.harpercollins.co.uk/green